Advanced Manufacturing
Strategy & Management

IFS

Advanced Manufacturing

Strategy & Management

Douglas K. Macbeth

IFS Publications, UK
Springer-Verlag
Berlin · Heidelberg · New York
London · Paris · Tokyo

Douglas K. Macbeth
Glasgow Business School
University of Glasgow
Glasgow G12 8LF

British Library Cataloguing in Publication Data

Macbeth, Douglas K.
  Advance manufacturing
  1. Manufacturing industries. Management
  I. Title
  658.5

ISBN 1-85423-039-5 IFS Publications
ISBN 3-540-51113-X Springer-Verlag Berlin Heidelberg New York Tokyo
ISBN 0-387-51113-X Springer-Verlag New York Heidelberg Berlin Tokyo

Commissioned and produced by **Technical Communications**, 100 High Avenue, Letchworth, Herts SG6 3RR

© 1989 **IFS Ltd,** 35-39 High Street, Kempston,
                Bedford MK42 7BT, UK
Springer-Verlag Berlin Heidelberg New York
                London Paris Tokyo

Phototypeset, printed and bound by Information Press Ltd, Eynsham, Oxford

For the three most important TLAs in my world –
AWM, GRM and CAM

CONTENTS

Preface

This book arose out of a number of precipitating factors. About eighteen months ago I was asked by Rick Creed of Cameron Iron Works to assist their management team develop a new manufacturing strategy. We determined that in order to prepare the ground we needed to be sure that everyone understood what was meant by all the TLAs (three letter acronyms) that were being banded about in the technical literature. There was a feeling that although most people were aware of the acronyms, there was a great danger that they meant different things to different people.

The first attempt at Chapters 3 and 4 were therefore directed at that group and I thank Rick and his team for the opportunity.

The second major factor was a series of extended conversations with Bob Barr of Cummins Engines, initially as part of our research project into "Buyer/Supplier Relationships in an AMT Environment."

We had already understood from many of the world-class companies we were dealing with in that project, that *quality, delivery* and *cost* were important but our research team were unclear as to the significance of sequence since different companies seemed to put them in a different order. We wondered if this might have some kind of internal significance in terms of priority of objectives.

It was Bob Barr who first demonstrated to me the logic of the sequence presented here. My thanks to him for his insight and patience.

I have also been fortunate to have had the opportunity to discuss these matters with a number of very smart and experienced managers on the MBA programme at the Glasgow Business School – so thanks to all of them.

Out of all this came the concept of this book: to return to basics and provide a means of evaluating Advanced Manufacturing Technology in a way which would be relevant to an individual company. It was also clear from work being done in the Centre for Technical and Organizational Change at GBS (CENTOC) that many companies were not obtaining full benefit from the introduction of new technologies and so the issues of implementation had also to be addressed.

To Mike Innes of Technical Communications thanks for his encouragement and assistance and to Irene Hood who has tried hard to recover my errors of typing input and grammar although no one can recover from errors or shortcomings in the text – mia culpa!

I have acknowledged Andrez Huczynski later in this book as well as David Boddy and Dave Buchanan of CENTOC. Glasgow is indeed fortunate to have these forward thinkers under one roof and I much enjoy being part of the team.

In all of my academic activity I try to work from the view that it must be useful to practising managers. If this book stimulates some thought about how we can better operate our manufacturing systems then I will be very satisfied but it really devolves to you to make the effort. I recognise that it is not always easy but I am encouraged by how much individual managers can do given the intelligence, the motivation, some crucial support from the top and an eagerness to improve their company's competitive situation.

Douglas K Macbeth

Introduction

This book is intended to help practising managers make sense of the choices available in manufacturing today.

The onset of global competition in most markets, the influx of more successful foreign competitors in formerly secure home markets and the pressures of drives to improve competitiveness are joined with major changes in the technologies of making and managing in manufacturing industry.

There is above all a need to get back to basics and identify what a particular manufacturing unit must be good at to support the higher business objectives. Advanced Manufacturing offers different routes to manufacturing excellence and these must be evaluated as to their contributions to providing the basic deliverables of all manufacturing businesses. This has to be done in ways which recognise the new objectives of working with much lower levels of inventory, with reducing lead times and with the avoidance of all other forms of waste, especially the waste of poor quality. Above all this has to be an ongoing process of continuous improvement.

Sense can be made of all of the acronyms of the new technologies if we consider how each can contribute to the needs expressed in the deliverables and the objectives. In this way we can provide the means of making choices in manufacturing which are consistent with a coherent strategy to provide support for those aspects of the business which allow us to win orders in the market place or which allow us simply to be a competitor.

All of this is difficult enough to do but the challenge really only then begins, for companies are living, dynamic organisations populated by people who are often averse to radical change. Yet radical change is what Advanced Manufacturing is all about.

We have a long way to catch up with the competition and they are not standing still!

The human and organisational aspects of new technology planning and implementation are crucial and the work developed at the Glasgow Business School provides a framework which helps effect a successful outcome.

The book's six main chapters follow the pattern outlined above.

Chapter 1 considers the manufacturing objectives which can be subsumed within the 'manufacturing deliverables' of *quality, delivery* and *cost*. *Quality* is the underpinning construct of the whole of manufacturing, *delivery* provides the heartbeat of the organisation and *cost* reduction follows success in the first two.

Chapter 2 provides a critical examination of principles which have been taught, accepted and put into practice but which can now be seen to be flawed. It then continues to suggest some new operational principles on which to base the design of a manufacturing system. These are considered to be more in line with current best practice.

Chapter 3 provides brief descriptions of a wide selection of Advanced Manufacturing Technologies and evaluates their contribution to satisfying the manufacturing deliverables. The relative cost benefit as well as cost reduction potential is also indicated.

Chapter 4 considers the nature of Corporate and Business Strategy which should inform and be informed by a suitable Manufacturing Strategy. Many AMTs are so extensive in their potential impact that a failure to consider these wider strategic concepts is almost certainly going to lead to problems later.

Chapter 5 recognises that many of the desirable features on offer through new technology fail to be fully appreciated or utilised because of problems of implementation. This chapter explores this situation and suggests the use of a decision framework already found to be of use by a number of organisations.

Chapter 6 provides examples of the problems that can arise by means of short case studies from companies involved in Advanced Manufacturing implementations. By highlighting these, we become more aware of the need for detailed preparations and ongoing activity.

The conclusion draws the discussion to a close by re-stating the new operating principles and the need, in the author's view, to take action in the manufacturing area. It seems absurd to believe that a trading nation can expect to build success on only services and invisibles when our population still demands more consumer goods and the Third World has requirements far in excess of provision for all kinds of manufactured produce.

Each chapter, except the last, begins with a statement of objectives to guide the thought process as you read and ends with a summary of the main points covered to try and help retention.

1 THE MANUFACTURING DELIVERABLES

The purpose of this chapter is to outline the basic requirements of any manufacturing business in terms of what it must do to support the business activities related to customer satisfaction and continued operation.

Specifically we shall be trying to fulfil the following objectives:

- Recognise that within a wide definition of *quality, delivery* and *cost*, we define the 'manufacturing deliverables'.

- Understand the underpinning role of *quality* as a solid foundation for all aspects of the business.

- Realise the importance of a favourable balance between supply lead time and customer demand lead time.

- Recognise that the supply chain relationship of supplier to customer applies to everyone.

● Realise that *cost* is an outcome, not neccessarily an input.

All manufacturing companies exist because they have identified and at least partially satisfied a set of customer requirements. They do this in a variety of ways using different product and process technologies which create their own management demands, problems and opportunities and, at least temporarily, they earn enough from their sales to permit reinvestment and continued trading.

This book will examine the underlying principles of operation of manufacturing businesses with a view to identifying the ways in which the variety of approaches grouped under the heading of Advanced Manufacturing Technology can contribute to a better and more strategic manufacturing capability.

Satisfaction of the internal and external customers is the key

Customer satisfaction with acceptable financial returns is the ultimate measure of business success. This obviously applies to the ultimate paying customer but there are also internal customers whose needs must be satisfied. In this way the whole business activity can be driven by customer satisfaction. Thus, manufacturing is purchasing's customer, final assembly is sub-assembly's, and so on through the whole chain of inter-connected and inter-dependent functional areas within the business.

We must recognise from the outset, therefore, that many of the things that are demanded of the manufacturing area can only be realised if other areas of the business also deliver their own form of customer satisfaction.

In general terms, a manufacturing business has to fulfil the requirements of the following statement:

Objectives

TO PROVIDE THE RIGHT PRODUCT, AT THE RIGHT TIME, AT THE RIGHT PLACE, TO THE SPECIFIED QUALITY LEVEL AT AN ACCEPTABLE COST.

These objectives also generate a series of other objectives, which should be considered as supporting the main ones. These are:

FLEXIBILITY, DELIVERY RELIABILITY, LEAD TIME AND INVENTORY STOCK LEVEL.

Fig. 1 demonstrates that there is a great deal of inter-connection between these objectives. The need to produce the right product at the right time creates a requirement to be flexible in the response to changing customer requirements. To get the product to the right place at the right time requires that

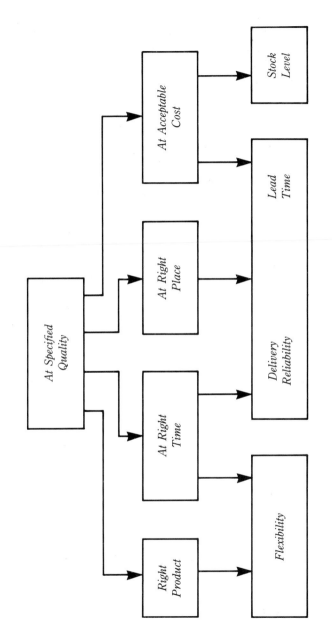

Fig. 1 Manufacturing objectives

delivery performance is reliable, and for some markets the length of time between a customer placing an order and its subsequent manufacture and delivery (i.e. lead time) becomes of interest. Acceptable cost comes through various effective uses of company resources to reduce the amount of time before the customer pays for the product (since the investment to produce the product is at risk for this time). One of the major risks is to have too much money tied up in stocks of material and so the level of such stock holdings becomes an important indicator of performance. Over-riding all of these is the absolute need to meet the precise requirement, i.e. to provide the specified quality. This is an over-arching requirement which impacts on each of the other objectives.

Quality is the overarching requirement

The above statement of the objectives of a manufacturing system is not, however, always easy to implement. In too many companies each of the areas with major responsibility for one or the other of the tasks sees only the immediate requirements of meeting its own idea of efficiency in its own operation. Too often this tendency is reinforced by management controls which do not necessarily reflect the true importance of the factors to be controlled. What is more important is that everyone in the company appreciates what the business is all about and makes every endeavour to ensure that the system as a whole continues to satisfy the final customer who, in the long run, decides if the business will survive.

One way of getting the message across about the true needs of the business is to realise that there is in fact a simple relationship between each of the objectives discussed above.

Manufacturing Deliverables: Quality, Delivery and Cost

This is what we can call the 'manufacturing deliverables', i.e. *quality, delivery and cost*. We will look at each of these in more detail, but at the moment it is enough to recognise the logic of the argument.

Quality is the underpinning of all that happens in manufacturing. Without control over *quality,* in all its many aspects, the business is forever fighting fires as they break out all over the company and is essentially in a damage limitation mode of operation.

Given a solid quality foundation to build on, the thing which then operates as the driver and initiator of action is the need to deliver to all of the customers along the chain, from basic raw material supply to final customer.

If *quality* is to specification and *delivery* is as planned, then what results is control of costs and therefore the capability to allow for attractive pricing of the product in the market place.

There are a number of new ways of thinking embodied in the last few statements.

It used to be thought, for example, that quality and cost were in opposition. That is to say that it was more costly to remove the last few points of bad quality, i.e. an example of the Law of Diminishing Returns in practice. Now we are realising that by proper control of quality at source, much unnecessary waste, and therefore cost, can be removed from the system. We therefore gain cost reductions, not by aiming for them directly, but by generating them as a consequence of doing the correct things.

Quality at source avoids many subsequent wastes

In like manner, it used to be regarded in British manufacturing that delivery was something that happened, eventually, whenever the production process had finally managed to get round to the product amid the chaos that best described the typical factory floor. By re-defining delivery to intermediate as well as final customers, we find a powerful tool to demonstrate the importance of each link in the chain. Delivery then becomes the heartbeat to keep material and information pumping round the system to ensure that all of the customers have all they need for their satisfaction.

Delivery is the heartbeat

Let us now look in more detail at each of these deliverables to see what each demands of our system and to set the scene for a consideration of how the various AMT approaches contributes to their performance.

QUALITY

Quality can be a difficult thing to define, since it can be tied to individual perceptions of value for money, as well as (perhaps not properly articulated) expectations of performance and appearance. Quality is also not limited only to the physical dimensions and performance of a product, but to a mix of product and service-related concepts packaged as a whole and offered to the customer for sale.

Quality is conformance to specification

In order to manage the process, it becomes necessary to specify quality as 'conformance to specification' and thereby shift the problem to the definition of the specification. Note that the specifications should be covering all of the extended requirements of the manufacturing system, since we must be able to specify the right product, the right time, the right place and the right or acceptable cost, as well as other aspects of customer service which might be reflected in aspects of flexibility, after sales service, considerate information processes and the more explicit marketing aspects relating to awareness of the company's products and services.

The first major specification exercise occurs at the interface between marketing and design.

New product ideas can come from two directions. They can come as a result of 'technology push' or by 'market pull'.

Market pull is often the more frequent one, where either existing customers recognise new requirements or modifications to existing products which would better satisfy them, or the company decides to mimic other companies' product offerings and perhaps incrementally improve on them, although often only superficially. Incrementalism is the essence of this approach and it can be a relatively low risk form of innovation, and one which can more easily be evaluated for financial returns based on the extrapolation of existing sales patterns. Many successful companies take this path and make a very good job of it. It is in many ways a very appropriate approach, since it requires sophisticated environmental scanning to ensure that customers and competitors are continually monitored to ensure that opportunities are not missed to make an improvement in the product portfolio.

Technology push operates from the opposite end of the supply chain. Here the innovative idea comes from the 'backroom', either from pure research or from development activities. The emphasis can be on a product or a process innovation for which there is no immediate customer requirement, but which is considered to have a major potential by its inventor. The question then becomes whether customers will value this as a better solution to the satisfaction of their existing needs, or whether a new customer need can be created to which this new product is suited. The difficulties of this approach are fairly obvious. There is no historical data to aid evaluation of potential market size or pricing policy, plus it is known that customers are very poor at evaluating the potential of a completely radical new product. Thus, such breakthrough types of innovation are extremely difficult to financially justify using traditional forms of investment appraisal and yet might actually have the capability to totally replace whole market sectors subject to incremental innovations.

Breakthrough innovations are difficult to justify in the short term, but may be more important in the longer term

Depending on the relative balance between these two forms of innovation, the manufacturing system can be required to do different things well by way of the detailed performance specifications of the system itself – but this does not deny the requirement to produce the manufacturing deliverables.

Wherever the source of the product idea, the need now is to establish the precise definition of everything that constitutes that product. Working from such a definition, the design function can then contribute its own originality to the definition and create the embodiment of the concept in a form suitable for manufacture.

It is at this stage that a great truism takes effect. That is that any quality lost at design cannot be put back at any other stage in manufacture. There is therefore a great responsibility on the designers to ensure that their design provides the functionality to perform the chosen task. This functionality is not just as the product leaves the factory doors, however. It must continue to function for the extent of its design life. In other words, *reliability* must also be designed into the product from the start. Traditionally, both of these activities have been recognised as the appropriate remit of the design team, but increasingly they are also required to investigate the details of how the product is to

Design for function, life and manufacture

be made and the ways in which the design of the product and the process can be made – to avoid creating quality problems for the manufacturing stages. These activities constitute a significant part of the first stage of a four part build up of quality cost: *prevention, appraisal, internal failure* and *external failure*.

The prevention stage includes, along with the above activities, aspects of planning, training and systems management, and *supplier quality assurance*. This latter activity is intended to provide an absolute guarantee that incoming material is totally conforming to the specification, thereby avoiding any need for costly verification and, of course, avoiding any quality problems in use.

The appraisal stage is the measurement phase where incoming material, part and finished product inspection, and product reliability testing take place. The costs incurred in this stage are relatively easy to establish, unlike the first one where different functional areas contribute to the process of specification generation. And it can be difficult to unravel the accounting system sufficiently to isolate the proportion which should be charged against quality-related activities.

Of the two failure areas, most people would be happy if they could restrict the problems to the internal category. Included here would be obvious items, like scrap, re-work, repair and re-test, but other action to define causes of failure and corrective actions, and any special efforts to improve performance, should also be accounted for in this category.

External failure costs related to warranty and customer complaint can be measured, but loss of customer support or goodwill as a result of poor quality cannot be directly quantified. Aspects of product liability costs can be counted here, but the efforts to design safe products, and thereby avoid liability problems, should probably be counted as a prevention cost.

Make quality prevention-driven

What has become very obvious in recent years is that Western producers have not been putting enough effort into the prevention category. Rather, they have tended to assume that the way to ensure that customers received adequate quality was to increase the appraisal costs and prevent the transmission of quality problems to the customer. (Note that such activities do not of themselves remove those factors responsible for creating the problem in the first instance and therefore it is guaranteed to recur at some future date.)

The cost of quality is likely to be greater than profits in traditional companies

There is therefore a great need to move away from a system in which failure is institutionalised into one which is prevention-driven. Although many companies need to make great efforts to find a believable figure for the actual costs incurred in failing to produce 'right first time', most evidence suggests that around 30% of the sales cost of the product can be accounted for by quality costs. If we consider that those same companies will be lucky if their profit margin measured the same way comes to double figures, we can see the real effects of control over quality.

Control over quality as it is produced has benefits to the whole organisation. Life is simpler with fewer crises if re-work or re-manufacture is avoided. Avoiding replacing failed parts reduces the complexity of production planning, as well as reducing the investment in working capital to finance the additional materials. Less 'fire-fighting' means fewer expensive 'fire-fighters', who often account for significant proportions of overhead, while not adding anything of direct value to the product. Such benefits can be best obtained by so organising and motivating everyone in the company to act as their own quality inspectors and improvers. In this way any waste of time, effort, materials, money and information can be recognised and subject to concentrated efforts to effect an improvement.

These kinds of activities apply equally well to indirect work areas as much as to direct production areas and may well have a much greater impact overall, given the often already reduced numbers employed in manufacture itself. Although averages do not describe any plant precisely, they indicate less than 20% of total cost to be direct workers, more than 50% in purchased materials, and the remainder as overhead. Control of these areas can also make life much simpler for the manufacturing area.

Within manufacturing itself we are beginning to listen to the same messages that were available for us to hear, but were apparently better understood by the Japanese. Quality at source is one of them, and probably the most important one; but another is to properly understand that it is processes much more than people that create the potential for poor quality. We therefore need to know what our processes are capable of and give that information to the designers, so that the dimensioning and tolerancing of the product can be done in the full knowledge that parts can come from the machine in a consistently satisfactory manner.

Processes, more than people, create the potential for good or bad quality

If the design can be specified such that the dimensions between the upper and lower tolerance bands is in excess of the normal expected range of dimensions produced by the process, then we can truly be said to have control at source. Fig. 2 indicates this desirable condition.

What remains, of course, is to monitor the process as it operates, to ensure that no extra influences have come to bear on the process, causing it to move away from its normal operation and into a zone where doubt about the resulting quality would begin.

This is the essential task assigned to Statistical Process Control, but total control over the process requires some supporting activities.

Total control over the process is the goal

Training of the process operations people in aspects of statistical methods is a recent development in the West, but is a feature of the Japanese success – having been at a high level of activity for more than three decades. These people also need

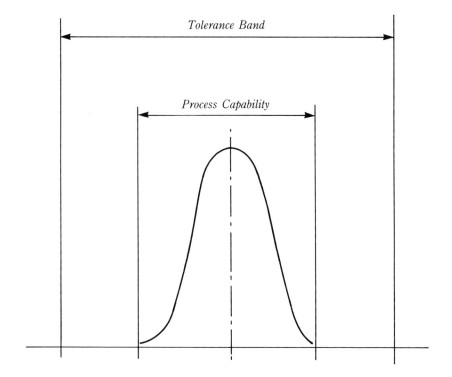

Fig. 2 Process capability and tolerance

to know the best places to apply the techniques (i.e. to the key quality and safety related factors) and to be provided with suitable equipment of a form geared to shop floor use and not reserved for skilled use by quality control staff away from the workplace. Maintenance of this specialised equipment, as well as the process itself, must also be a major factor, and this must be properly planned and implemented. In many cases, the way in which a process is set up to operate can create waste of itself and attention must be directed as a priority to improvements here which will not only reduce scrap but affect delivery performance as well.

To support all of this, the information systems must be fully thought out and, again, properly implemented and improved on as circumstances evolve. The final thread is to have total control over the quality of the materials coming into each area. Within the same plant, upstream SPC provides such confidence, but many companies depend on a number of supplier companies to provide a variety of components and assemblies. This is why Supplier Quality Assurance programmes are so important and it is significant that the more developed of these are more interested in the capability of the supplier's process than merely its ability to 'inspect in' a level of conformance to specification.

Identifying the cost of quality requires new measures

There can be little doubt that quality is not free, but equally the cost of 'unquality' is, in most cases, a lot more than had been appreciated, and usually a lot more than had been measured before the accountants were given better specification of what they should be delivering.

Quality, therefore, truly is everyone's business in the company. This is not, however, another of those slogans without the necessary follow through as we used to have from time to time in our manufacturing companies. Rather, this is a recognition of the centrality of quality at source for every activity throughout office and factory and through the supply chain into and out of the plant. Only by doing this will we have any chance of competing against the best in the world.

Quality is a moving target

There is one further problem, however. Just as it can be difficult to define quality, it is further complicated by the fact that the target to aim for is not static. Increased customer expectations and competitors' actions to gain an advantage, mean that we must be constantly upgrading our performance against an aggressive target and then, as we approach closer to it, we must move it further away again. This is not culturally something which Westerners find completely natural, but our competitors are happy with a concept of a continuing journey to self-improvement. They have already shown that they are not content to obtain 99.9% quality levels. Rather, they re-define the measurement system to reflect the new targets and count parts per million which fail. (N.B. 100 parts per million is equivalent to 0.01%)

People can be a source for improvements

Here again we can see a major change in traditional Western attitude is required to accept the challenge of striving for the receding target. It can be done, however, and companies report incredible improvements achieved through the involvement of all of their people in improvement activities, which not only provide improving quality but also better working conditions and more interesting work for the participants.

Let us now turn our attention to the other main deliverable, *delivery* itself.

DELIVERY

Delivery is a contract between parties, such that a certain quantity of specified items are to be made available by the first party at a specified time and location in suitable containers, such that the second party can make use of them. Sometimes this contract is in the form of a legal arrangement duly endorsed and binding. At other times, the arrangement is completely informal between peers within one company. The formal contracts are normal between companies and their suppliers and between companies and their customers, but for the total system to function properly the same level of concern needs to be applied to the internal contract as should be paid to the external ones.

Of the above factors encompassed in the delivery concept most can be specific to a particular customer, but some negotiation is also possible. The items ordered may be to some extent customised for a particular requirement, or may be standard for all customers. Increasingly, customers are specifying specific forms of goods packaging to avoid any need to re-pack or count incoming goods. In similar fashion, the destination of the goods is now more variable. The actual time of delivery is becoming more precise. Former practice would have been to agree a delivery week and allow the supplier to determine for himself when in the week delivery would take place. Sometimes, in fact, it was the transportation company who had the final decision, but not in the more advanced companies today.

The excess time that can be built into delivery times is another example of reducible waste worthy of major effort.

On-time delivery is a basic requirement

The time aspects of delivery thus have two major components. The first is the actual agreed time to deliver. This is, in fact, the more important factor, since we have already established that companies exist in a complex sequence of interacting buyer/supplier relationships. As a result of this, each purchaser is dependent on satisfactory delivery service from its supplier, otherwise its own performance will be compromised. To avoid such close coupling in the past, companies would hold stocks of material as a buffer against the things which always seemed to go wrong. Such stockholdings are now regarded as another waste of resource to be minimised. The interdependence has not been eliminated, however. Rather, it has been enhanced, making an absolute requirement to perform against the specified delivery date – and this to be done in a totally reliable and con-

Delivery into the 'window' must be consistently reliable

sistent manner. Supplier companies can be subject to delivery agreements which will specify a very small 'window' within which they will be allowed to deliver. This will usually permit some (little) amount of early delivery, but absolutely no late delivery. Whether there are immediate financial penalties for failure against the supplier or not, there is little doubt that such performance will not be permitted to be the norm.

The second component of time-related delivery is the length of time taken between notification of the requirement to deliver and actual delivery. This we can call the 'demand lead time'. This will obviously vary according to the form of the business. In a 'make to stock' situation, customers would expect to have the product available off-the-shelf with effectively zero demand lead time. In a 'make to customer order' situation, the customer will have an expectation of how long he might be expected to have to wait for supply of the goods. This expectation is subject to many influences, both from the past history of the supplier and also from the actions of possible competitors in the supply market. It is also likely that the customer has his own customer, who might well be exercising his right to demand better response times, and the effect ripples back through the supply chain. A capability to offer a reduced time to process an order might therefore offer the chance of a competitive edge in the market place, but the prime importance still has to be placed on actually achieving the required delivery date whatever it is.

In essence, what is required is absolute control over delivery performance and then an improvement in the ability to produce at short notice. Whether a company chooses to make such an ability a major part of its strategy is a more complex decision – since once short delivery can be achieved, the likelihood is that this becomes the norm and the temporary advantage is lost.

Internal customers must be served just as reliably as external ones

Within any one company absolute performance to customer requirement is still paramount, except that the customer is now simply the next production stage. What should not be a problem is to recognise that reducing the delivery response time must be good for the business. However, the sequence of reaching these objectives remains the same.

Delivery can also include within its remit the need to provide a variety of *flexibilities* to the customer. Flexibility can be needed to cope with changing customer requirements for product variety. This might be from within an existing range of standard products, or might involve a re-design or modification to

Customers expect a flexible reaction to their changing requirements

semi-standard products. The effort to make a change might therefore require work to be done at all stages of the manufacturing process. The most extreme example of this is the need to introduce a totally new product to satisfy either an expressed customer requirement or a strategic requirement to enter a new part of the market.

Within existing product ranges, flexibility can still be required to accept the need to deliver different quantities at different times, or to accept the possibility of producing a mix of product types for delivery together. Here, again, inventory holdings can cover this requirement, but at a cost. That cost might, however, be necessary if the cost of providing flexibility is much greater.

We must recognise that problems appear for a manufacturer with any move to increase or decrease quantity or product type. An increase in demand requires that sufficient materials can be made available in sufficient time to process them and deliver. Material supply may be dependent on a supply chain of other companies whose reaction time must also be taken into account. In like fashion, a decrease can mean that production is cut off sooner than planned, but what about the supply orders already in the pipeline? Can they be switched off as quickly? It is likely that they cannot. For companies ordering from Far Eastern suppliers, for example, a six week sea journey means that much more than that quantity is at risk by a reduced requirement. This factor can also be a consideration for new product introductions in trying to establish an optimum time to stop ordering the old parts and switching orders to the new. In highly dynamic product markets, supply contracts might prove not to be well-founded as actual market demands are experienced, and there has to be a way of managing the suppliers to provide for the required output variations.

To try and put this in a framework for discussion, let us examine what we can call the 'supply/demand balance'. We have already described the demand lead time, now we need to develop a measure of the total time taken to supply a complete product to satisfy a customer requirement.

The balance between supply and demand lead times measures the risks and responses of manufacture

Fig. 3 illustrates this concept. The total time to supply a product is made up of more or less sequential sets of activities. Working from right to left in the diagram, we recognise the time to deliver the finished goods to the customer. Prior to this comes the manufacture stage, which could run all the way through from basic product idea, through design and production test and pack

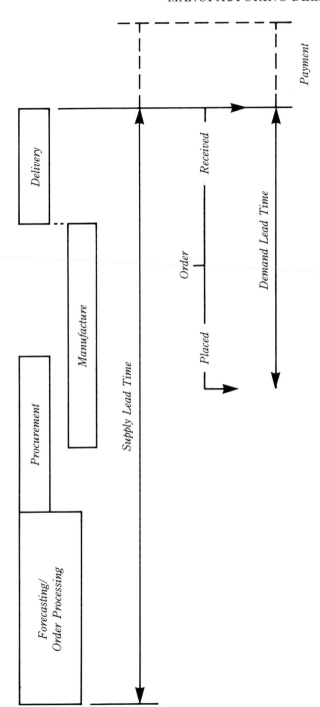

Fig. 3 Supply/demand balance

stages. In order to produce, some source materials are likely to be required, and so we have to work back through another company's supply lead time – 'procurement'.

The first part of the sequence depends on the form of the business. If the company is only producing to customer order, then this part of the total is largely taken up by the time taken to process the order. In fact, this may be quite complicated, as the company tries to fully understand the specification and then pass this to design in the manufacture stage. If the company cannot afford to wait for the actual order to materialise, it is forced to forecast a certain level of demand in order to start the process moving in time to react to the order when it finally comes. Of course, the real world can be more complicated than this. Often it is necessary to place orders on suppliers long before any detailed forecasts can be made, or orders processed simply because the company needs to get into the queue for critical components. Some electronics components are like this.

The point of this is to recognise the degree to which a business is at risk through not having an acceptable balance between supply lead time and demand lead time.

In effect, any time in excess of the demand lead time which is necessary for the supply side operations constitutes a hazard area for the company. Investment will be required here whether it be in purchase order costs, or design department overhead, or working capital costs, or whatever. All of these things are at risk until the product is delivered and payment is received.

It is obvious, therefore, why delivery is so important, but also so dependent on many different parts of the total supply chain system.

As long as the supply lead time is much greater than the demand lead time, then risk investment is required. In fact, the larger is the supply lead time the more we are forced into forecasting over a longer period. This of itself, increases the risk factor. The ideal situation would, of course, be where supply lead time was less than the demand lead time, since here no speculative purchasing or production would be needed prior to the receipt of the firm order. Such a system would offer the ultimate in flexibility and still be economical to operate.

Consideration of Fig. 3 also indicates the two-edged nature of allowing customers the opportunity to specify a reduced demand lead time. With no action taken on the supply side, such a change simply increases the investment at risk and the cost of financing it. It is no surprise to learn of typical supplier reactions to large companies who are moving to 'Just-in-Time' approaches to manufacture necessitating more frequent deliveries in smaller quantities, that this is simply an attempt to make the supplier hold the buyer's inventory and shift the risk back towards the supplier.

From this framework of *quality* and *delivery*, we come to the outcome – *cost*.

COST

Cost is one measure of resource use which, because it is in the units in which businesses keep their 'scores', has been regarded as one of the major factors used by companies to manage the manufacturing area. For many years the main responsibility of manufacturing management was to control costs. This is not surprising given the very high proportion of total company assets of all kinds which are utilised in a typical manufacturing business. Nevertheless, this orientation towards control overlooked the very real contribution which manufacturing could offer towards profit generation through supporting a properly thought out strategy.

'Control' of cost is not the primary target for manufacturing

It should also be realised that cost is an internal measure and is not immediately relevant to a customer in the same way as quality and delivery. Of course, the manifestation of cost can be in a product price to a customer, but there is not a direct link between the two items. Pricing is a feature of what the market will bear, while appropriate cost can facilitate the possibility of competitive pricing by providing a margin in which such decisions can comfortably be made.

A failure to recognise the separation between cost and price has led in the past to the kind of nonsense where a dictate from, for example, the financial controller, to cut costs by 10% across the board is seen as a quick way to increased competitiveness. In reality, such approaches often failed because the lack of competitiveness was not uniformly distributed across the whole operation, but may well have come from an area where some additional short-term spending may have so changed the complete system behaviour that reductions in cost much greater than 10% could then have been achieved!

Overall cost reductions can come from increased expenditure in some areas

Quality is a perfect example of this. We have already discussed how increased spending at the prevention stage reduces the appraisal and failure costs later.

It is therefore necessary to recognise that cost is a result of other actions to use or not use particular resources. Cost is in effect built up of necessary resources utilised in production of the finished product to the current specification, plus a measure of wasted resource built in because the system has not been smart enough to avoid their use. These wastes of themselves should be subject to the same quality improvement activities as any other area within the company.

Removing waste reduces cost and simplifies the process

The aim of all business should be to remove as much waste as possible and continue to look for ways in which the base requirement for resources is also reduced. Such approaches are doubly virtuous.

Reducing costs reduces the risks involved in being in business by reducing the amounts to be financed, while at the same time providing Marketing with a greater opportunity to offer attractive terms to customers.

Cost reduction therefore has to be a major objective of any business, but of itself is little more than a convenient measurement scale against which the improvement path can be plotted.

There remains a major difficulty, which is only now being recognised by the accounting profession. That is a recognition that traditional cost accounting methods often make it difficult to make the important decisions about future management actions. What has happened is that accounting standards and procedures have grown up, or have developed, over many years to suit perceived requirements at that time. They have also tended to reinforce a short-term view of performance in support of favourable stock market reaction. This form of company evaluation produces a kind of surreal business scene where the companies can be considered almost to exist as money machines rather than product producers and customer satisfiers.

New approaches to cost accounting are needed

There are signs of new approaches to accounting to recognise the importance of manufacturing method and the effects on longer term market share and future volumes of production, as well as moves to make appropriate allowances for the difficult to quantify but important considerations which impact on investment decision.

Cost therefore must be allocated its proper role in the business.

Like the other *deliverables*, it must be properly specified, measured and improved upon, but let us not again fall into the trap of thinking of cost as the driver of the business. It is a scorekeeper, and an internal one at that.

SUMMARY

- The Manufacturing Deliverables are *quality, delivery* and *cost*
- Quality is the foundation on which success is built
- Quality is *conformance to specification*
- Customer's requirement along the supply chain is the specification
- The cost of quality is a measure of how well or how badly you are doing
- Quality at source is primarily dependent on the design and the process, but people and systems make it work
- Quality improvement is a continuous journey towards perfection
- Reliable delivery comes first, short delivery can be an advantage
- Ideal manufacturing would have the supply lead time less than the demand lead time
- Risk increases with increased gap between supply lead time and demand lead time
- Delivery by all suppliers to all customers along the supply chain is the heartbeat for the business
- Cost is an outcome of actions, not an input
- Cost is a measure of waste and has to be continuously reduced

2 A NEW WAY OF THINKING

In this chapter we consider the ways in which the *manufacturing deliverables* can be achieved. To do this we firstly challenge some of the 'taken for granted' assumptions or approaches once taught as the only truths which we are slowly realising are not serving the new competitive situation. We then build up new patterns of thought more in tune with current best practice in manufacturing.

The two basic objectives of this chapter are therefore to:

- Critically evaluate the 'received wisdoms' of traditional manufacturing.

- Develop new guiding principles for manufacturing which satisfy the identified business needs of the new situation.

The question we must address is why it has become necessary to reappraise what we are doing in manufacturing management.

It seems almost to have come as a surprise to find that in many markets we have become very uncompetitive, and yet in the UK we started the first Industrial Revolution, and in the USA we have for long had a role model for management practice. This latter position we now find has been taken by the Japanese, and many managers and scholars now make the pilgrimage to see what secrets there are to be obtained and applied to produce instant success. What is now obvious is that quick fixes in only limited areas of the business are simply not good enough.

Japan must export sufficiently to pay for its essential imports of raw materials, but then the UK has also been a major exporter since the Industrial Revolution, only going into deficit on its manufacturing trade for the first time in 1983.

So, what is the secret of the Japanese success? What it is not on average is 'the factory of the future'. Rather, it is what one American manager described as the factory of the present, operating as it should and could do if the same attention to detail and commitment to the future were to be transferred back home.

The factory of the present requires attention to detail and commitment to the future

When the Japanese began in the late 1950s to examine how they could improve their industrial performance, they turned to Western examples for guidance. These examples were also there for Western managers to learn from, but for some reason this did not happen. Particularly in the area of quality, where Japan had a terrible reputation, American academics had a major influence in shaping their industrial practices. The names of Deming, Juran and Feigenbaum are well known and their writings well received, understood and developed. In the UK at least this did not happen until recently as managers came to terms with the Japanese example.

Why should this be? In the UK there has long been no effective provision for the continuing education of manufacturing managers and their employees, many of whom are already less well qualified than even their continental equivalents. Add to this a social climate where the role and status of the engineering profession has been the subject of a number of national enquiries but only limited impact, and where at the start of the 1980s it was still possible to make the point that we graduated more people in the Welsh language than in Production Engineering.

Unquestioning, repetitive management approaches are no longer adequate

Such an attitude produces a tendency to create forms of industrial organisation that have 'take for granted' approaches, which served adequately in former less competitive times, and institutionalise them in procedures and policies which can be operated in an unquestioning and repetitive fashion.

A further problem drawn from American experience is seen as a short-term focus, especially in financial matters allied to a poor realisation of the need for innovation at the product and process levels.

The statements below give examples of some of the received wisdoms which have so shaped our behaviour to date, but which, if critically examined, point us in a more productive direction.

CHALLENGING RECEIVED WISDOMS

- *Inventory is an asset*

  NO – It is a liability. It may appear on the balance sheet as an asset, but only on the assumption that the inventory can be sold. Often this will require more expenditure to finish the product, and in the meantime all of the extra material makes it more difficult to produce what is actually required. Inventory can be an opportunity, however, since by its reduction, comes improvements in the visibility of problems and a reduction in operating capital requirements, which can be re-deployed to better use.

- *Set-up times force large batch sizes*

  YES – if you do nothing about them! Note, however, that the formula which gives the batch size that balances the costs of setting-up against the cost of holding stock, also provides a clue to a different solution.

$$\text{Economic Batch Quantity} = \sqrt{\frac{2 \times \text{set-up cost} \times \text{usage}}{\text{holding cost}}}$$

This shows that, as set-up costs tend towards zero, then the EBQ also tends towards zero. Thus, faced with the same equation, Western managers have accepted it at face value and calculated large batch sizes as a norm; whereas the

Japanese have taken the view that they wanted smaller batch sizes and therefore the set-up cost had to be reduced. So successful have they been that, in terms of time, there are examples of reductions from several hours to under ten seconds, and the aim is effectively instantaneous set-up and change-over times.

- *Quality and cost are in opposition*

NO – By improving quality, cost is reduced, but only if the quality effort is properly directed. Make the system prevention driven not failure driven.

- *Long lead times mean we need better forecasts*

YES – but no one can forecast accurately and in detail a long time ahead. If we reduce the lead time the forecast accuracy is less of a problem.

- *High product variety is difficult for manufacturing to manage*

YES – but if the customers want it, we have to make it possible. We need flexibility in the process and in our people, and we need to design for manageable variety and minimum lead time.

- *An idle resource is an inefficiency and is not paying its way*

YES – but if the *total system effectiveness* is improved, then the business is better for it. If it has done all that is required of it, it has paid its way – now use it for other required or developmental activities.

- *People are a resource to be managed like any other*

NO – People are the means to a better future. They are the major thing which differentiates companies – most other things can be purchased. If all you purchase are people's presence without their intellect and interest, you are wasting your money.

- *There is a cycle of managerial requirement – quality, then cost, then production output, and so it goes on*

NO – Successful companies do not change directions like this. They want it all at once and no trade-offs. (Consistent with market requirements.)

- *Scrap is always present – factor in an appropriate allowance*

NO – Why must it always be present? If the factor goes in, you control against the factor and think you are doing a good job, but there is no improvement.

Given that these are only some examples of challenges to the received wisdoms, what does this mean for companies?

Firstly, we should set-up a programme to surface all the 'taken for granted' assumptions that exist in our organisations. In each department there will be things that are done for the simple reason that they have always been done that way, e.g. tolerancing in design, overhead allocation in costing, batch sizing in purchasing, etc.

Surface the received wisdoms

By approaching each assumption in a totally naive, questioning way, we can perhaps brainstorm our way through the mental road-blocks. In fact, it may be a good organisation trick to ask one person from a particular area to establish the assumptions for another area. In this way he learns about another area, since he will be naive enough, but smart enough, to ask interesting questions and, at the same time, we will begin to penetrate some of the functional departmental defence barriers and begin to build a team for the future.

Check the validity for the whole organisation

By surfacing the 'taken for granted' assumptions, we are now in a position to examine critically their validity for current operations. Above all, it is important to ask questions about the utility of these things from the viewpoint of the complete company and not simply from one departmental view. For this reason we must question what other departments' activities are affected by these assumptions. Only if they are valid from the wider viewpoint can they justify retention, but not for ever. We must also institute a system of periodic review, so that inappropriate practices do not creep in by default at a later date.

As a guide to the kinds of thinking which we should use to help this process, let us now develop a new set of approaches which emerge from the challenges already discussed.

NEW APHORISMS IN MANUFACTURING

1. Customers are your future – get close to them

We have established that customer satisfaction is what business is all about if it is to survive in a competitive environment, but how do we know what will constitute satisfaction if we do not make the effort to understand our customers. They are subject to all sorts of pressures from external changes in the environment which can impact their expectations of us, or their evaluation of our performance. It is not enough to leave this to the sales or marketing people as part of their normal jobs, the need is much greater than that.

Manufacturing needs the very best information of changing customer requirements to have any chance of satisfying their demands, and the closer the relationship the more the efforts will be seen to be in support of a person to whom one can relate, rather than another number in an order book. This does not mean that the traditional customer contact people are no longer required, but simply that more people need to understand the customer. It is possible that more people will be in contact about a variety of matters, e.g. quality, production planning, design and packaging, distribution, etc. This can create its own problems, of course, if too many are tramping all over the customer's premises and not getting the work done at base; but electronic data transmission can help the information flow once the personal contacts have been established.

2. Provide a flexible response to customers' needs

Closeness to a changing requirement is not much use if you cannot make the requisite changes to your production output. Production systems therefore need to be designed to cater for much greater levels of variety of volume and product mix, as well as increased rates of new product introduction. This variety capability can be provided by hardware and software systems, but the people in the business must also be flexible in the kind of work they are equipped to do and perhaps also in their attendance pattern at work.

Increasing flexibility to respond is a result of reducing the total supply time, as discussed in Chapter 1, and so the system designers must examine each aspect of that measure to obtain improvement.

3. Suppliers are your life blood – nurture them

A major part of most total supply lead times is the time taken by your suppliers to respond to the changes you make. They may well wish to follow Lesson 1, but even if they have not fully understood what is entailed, there is still a responsibility on you to provide them with the information to do the job properly. In some cases this will involve providing education and technical support until their own level of capability improves, and may also involve providing equipment or calibration facilities for quality improvements to be made. Suppliers can also contribute to design studies in their own areas of expertise, which can result in products more precisely engineered to our requirements and also easier for the supplier to manufacture – since any production difficulties have been designed out at an early stage.

A closer involvement with suppliers can provide longer term cost reductions as the team work begins to take effect in redesign and value analysis exercises.

4. Take a total systems viewpoint – along the whole supply chain

It has been a feature of Western companies to go for rather narrow specialisations in the kinds of jobs that we ask people to do. This has had the effect that few have been able to take a sufficiently broad view of what the business really needed to do to be competitive. The systems approach suggests that the interconnectedness of different bits of the business activity means that decisions made in one area impact on activities in other less obvious ones. The analogy used to be made with a stone dropped into a pond and the ripples moving through and back across the surface. Perhaps a more up-to-date one would be the effect of a change in one cell of a complex spreadsheet. Here again there is a rippling effect, but the relationships can be as complex as we choose to put into the formulae determining the content of each cell address.

We must have a model or structure of our whole business and a complete understanding of the paths and flows of information and cause/effect relationships. This creates the need for different training and skills of participants in the company, as well as more developed awareness of the purpose of the business and how it can be achieved.

One of the useful features of systems theory is the option to define where the boundary lies between internal and external influences. For the same reasons as before, the system must now consider the effects of an extended supply chain on eventual customer satisfaction. This does not mean that companies must aim necessarily for increased vertical integration, since often this can divert companies away from their areas of competence and distinctive capability and lead to calls to 'get back to the knitting'. Rather, it recognises the dependence of many buyer/supplier relationships all the way along the chain. The effects of failures of these relationships on total system performance has to be recognised and suitable management approaches put in place to safeguard customer satisfaction.

5. Aim for effectiveness – not efficiency

Efficiency has a simple definition as the ratio of output to input and is often easy to calculate. The difficulty comes in the way we have tended to apply this measure. If applied to narrowly defined areas of activity, this measure can give good results, but looked at from a wider viewpoint, less satisfactory results are seen. A prime example would be national productivity measures defined in efficiency terms as the ratio of manufactured goods produced to numbers employed. This has the interesting result that, as long as the numbers employed are falling faster than the rate at which actual production is reducing, then productivity is said to be rising. Of course, such a pattern cannot continue for ever, since we could be highly efficient at producing very little indeed.

Efficiency measures also have the disadvantage that their requirement for precision in measurement of the values used means that we tend to use such approaches to monitor only those things which are easy to measure, rather than those it would be best to measure. As a result, we have concentrated on measures of labour utilisation (equivalent hours of produced goods : input hours of people as recorded by attendance clocks) without spending enough effort on determining whether the output was in fact the correct output, i.e. actually demanded by a customer. In similar fashion, traditional accounting practice suggests that expensive capital equipment must recover its investment by continual operation, thereby spreading the overhead over more units of output. But if this means that the production flow is unbalanced and that we are producing parts for which there is no immediate requirement, we are simply making the job harder for ourselves and tying up money in a form in which it is more difficult to gain a return through actual sales.

Narrowly focused 'efficiency' thinking also leads to the crime of sub-optimisation. This occurs when one area takes what can be regarded as an optimum decision from its own perspective, but in so doing makes it more difficult for another area to make a move which would actually provide a greater benefit to the complete system. An example could be a production manager thinking (perhaps because the company reward system supports the view) that he should be aiming for lower unit costs and, as a result, buys specialised equipment that produces lower unit costs, but only if kept fully utilised. In the meantime the marketing function recognises a new market opportunity, but one which requires a more flexible response and therefore less consistent use of the new inflexible equipment. Such things are not unusual and many companies have suddenly woken up to the fact that their existing factories are simply not appropriate for the current market situation, and yet the sclerosis was so gradual that it was not realised for years.

We therefore have a need for a measure of performance which can build on existing ones, but is focused on what is required of the total system and not simply sub-sets of it.

A suitable concept is *total system effectiveness*, where the effort is to so specify performance standards on the major parameters of the business that these become an overarching framework within which narrower measures can still play a part. The *manufacturing deliverables* of Chapter 1 can provide such global concepts.

Notice, however, one corollary to this. It may well be the case that in order for the higher level measures to be satisfactory an area may be forced to make a distinctly less than ideal decision locally to ensure the attainment of the superior goals. This possibility must be recognised in the ways that individual performance is monitored, for in our culture at least the individual owes at least as much loyalty to himself as to the organisation. A change from efficiency to effectiveness will need a very thorough-going review of many organisational practices to ensure that the change actually sticks and becomes the normal mode of operation.

6. Simplicity before complexity – people before machines

There is perhaps an understandable attraction in being able to respond to difficult and complex situations in manufacturing and a real sense of achievement in putting out the fires of crises, but the question should be asked why the fire was there in the first place.

Very often it is because we have not taken a systems view

and have failed to design our business activity to function in a controlled, logical way. It is relatively easy to fall into the trap of trying to be all things to all people. The danger is that in so trying, we create a structure which is so complex that it becomes increasingly difficult to manage and its very complexity means that, in fact, we end up not satisfying any customer's requirement.

The human brain can only cope with a limited amount of data at a time before overloading, and so manufacturing systems, which are supposed to cope with highly complex situations, end up being dependent on computer aids to decision making. By definition, however, the brain cannot cope with the multiple decision streams, and so people are often disenfranchised by the very computer which is supposed to be there to help them. Perhaps expert or knowledge-based systems will make a difference, but not yet.

Computer systems also have their own requirements, which make demands on the human interfaces in terms of data accuracy and timeliness. This creates additional disciplines for which training must be given. This, of course, presumes that the computer system actually has the capability to perform the task for which it was designed. The evidence from the workplace is that this is not always the case and, in any event, if the market place is changing as fast as we have been indicating, then the system should also change.

Thus, before getting locked into a complex solution to a complex problem, firstly establish whether the problem could not be simplified. Simple situations might be amenable to human-scale solutions monitored by human-based reporting and control structures inherently more adaptable in a shorter timescale.

Many have reported the majority of benefits in automation projects coming well before any automation was installed and 80% of the benefit for 20% of the cost is typical. If this is generally the case, then we should be looking for the simple solution as a first objective. It may well be that for reasons of consistency and accuracy a machine may in the end prove to be the appropriate choice, but the human intellect, suitably trained and motivated, can produce dramatic insights into most processes and can significantly improve performance.

Many advanced technologies fall into the 'coping with complexity' category and, while they will have a role to play, it must be tailored to the needs of the business and not done for its own sake. If this is not the case, they might provide further examples of sub-optimisation, as discussed in the last section.

7. Design for function, form and effective manufacture

Designers have a crucial part to play in any successful manufacturing business. We have already discussed their interface with customer specifications, but they are also creative in their own right. It is perhaps another artificial division to separate out these three areas where design decisions are critical, but many organisations have done just that.

Function was established by the engineering design team and their concepts were then passed to industrial engineers, whose task was to decide how the thing could be made. The form or aesthetic appearance of the product might have been passed to an industrial designer who, again, might not have detailed knowledge of manufacturing methods, problems and capabilities.

Such differentiation of responsibility makes control difficult and can create new problems in extending the timescale of the total design task. Some of the AMTs are making it possible to approach the situation where one designer can perform all of these related tasks, but this does not remove the need for an understanding of the design task in a much wider role than has been normal.

One of the obvious ways of offering variety to customers, while at the same time not creating impossible tasks for the business to manage, is to go for a modular design approach. Here the variety is created by the ways in which the final product is built up from its standard component sub-systems. Such a design approach requires a very full understanding of the market requirements and how they might change, plus a manufacturing process capable of producing the variety effectively. In terms of the system logistics, the later the specialised parts - which provide the customer specified uniqueness - can be left before adding to the product structure, the easier it will be to manage the supply chain.

We have already discussed the importance of designing quality and reliability into the product. In the same way, the means of setting-up machines to produce can be influenced by careful design. Yet another aspect will be to so design mating parts that they can only be assembled in the correct orientation and thereby remove at source one possible cause of a quality problem.

8. Avoid waste – add value, not cost

Waste occurs in three main forms - time, money and effort. We can define waste as any resource expended in excess to that actually required and valued by the customer. Of course, it will not always be easy to identify the minimum required standard of value that should be added to a product as it passes through a particular stage of manufacture, but that is the task.

We can think of waste being introduced into the planning process through excessive lead-times, into the product by attempts to over-engineer the design, into the process by bad management practice, and into the general overhead by the growth of peripheral activities which may be nice to have but in fact do not contribute greatly to customer satisfaction. Care needs to be taken, however, that the accounting is done in an intelligent manner. Many British companies have a history of seeing training and development as such an overhead to be cut at the first turndown in trading performance.

What needs to be established is what it is that the company actually contributes to customer satisfaction and then to establish what functions in what form are required to provide that in a wholly satisfactory manner. Viewed in this light, each person's contribution can be examined to see what effect they are having on creating the right kind of output, or in minimising the amount of input resources needed for that output.

The concentration on value also demonstrates an outward focus towards the customer rather than an inward cost-limiting one – which might result in reduced cost but proportionately greater reduced value to the customer. This is another example where traditional accounting procedures need to be re-examined to ensure that we are measuring that which is important to measure.

One of the biggest wastes is unnecessary inventory, and efforts to reduce that often releases investment to tackle other wastes.

9. Do it once and do it right

One of the obvious wastes is a failure to perform according

to the specification. This creates a need to do it again, or rectify the mistake, or perhaps undo later actions to correct this earlier fault. Such events waste all kinds of resources and interfere with business objectives, while often creating pressures for more overhead to monitor, control or rectify the failings. In product manufacture, this means putting responsibility and ability at the place of creation, and this also applies across the organisation. Every person should know precisely what is required of them and should commit to providing their output fault free. This may be a standard of perfection, but why not?

10. Aim for continuous improvement

Business is a competitive situation. If our competitors are perceived by our customers to be doing a better job than we are in satisfying their needs, then it may not be long before they are no longer our customers. On the other hand, a customer who perceives us as trying always to improve, may be prepared to tolerate some slight lack of competitiveness while we take time to put new systems into place. Such a relationship with a customer can actually provide a real barrier to entry into our marketplace and is much to be desired.

The biggest danger is complacency. It is quite normal for artists, musicians and other performers, as well as craftsmen, to have a personal drive to improve their skills which is inner directed and provides satisfaction to the person, almost irrespective of whether the world at large recognises that development process. What we need to engender in our manufacturing businesses is that same pride in performance and striving to excel which we see and admire in other activities. It may not always be possible for wage earners to identify so closely with a company's success as an owner might, but work still plays a large part in how people are perceived in our society and the positive feelings of contributing to the success of our organisation can be a motivator in itself.

We have now seen that the manufacturing scene is subject to more questioning than at any time over the past several decades. The old guiding principles are being found not to cope with the new competitive situations, and new ways of thinking are being embodied in technologies and management approaches which aim to correct these failings. In the next chapter we will look at the role of the Advanced Manufacturing Technologies in satisfying the new requirements.

SUMMARY

- Customers are your future – get close to them
- Provide a flexible response to customer needs
- Suppliers are your life blood – nurture them
- Take a total systems viewpoint – along the whole supply chain
- Aim for effectiveness not efficiency
- Simplicity before complexity – people before machines
- Design for function, form and effective manufacture
- Avoid waste – add value, not cost
- Do it once and do it right
- Aim for continuous improvement

3 CONTRIBUTION FROM ADVANCED MANUFACTURING TECHNOLOGIES

In this chapter we will describe briefly the main features of some AMTs and highlight the ways in which they contribute to the major manufacturing deliverables of *quality, delivery* and *cost*. The total list will be split into two sections. The first will deal with hardware-based technologies, while the second deals with systems or software-based approaches.

In any attempt like this to encapsulate a rapidly changing field, there is the likelihood of missing something (we will not, for example, spend much time on actual process technologies for the reason that such improvements as are provided can easily be evaluated against the same criteria discussed here). For those AMTs not covered, a critical evaluation along the same paths used here should make apparent their possible contributions to system effectiveness.

The main objectives of this chapter are therefore to :

- Describe the basic nature of a number of AMTs.
- Consider how each AMT contributes to *quality, delivery* and *cost* reduction.
- Assess, in a qualitative fashion, the possible balance of benefit against the relative expense of the investment.

HARDWARE-BASED TECHNOLOGIES

Automated Guided Vehicles (AGVS)

An AGV is a material transfer solution for parts or tooling which must be moved to visit a number of discrete processing stations in a manufacturing route. This often involves parts being accurately positioned on a pallet, which is also transferred at each process stage. It can be guided by following painted lines on the floor or by tracing the path of a conductor cable buried in the floor. Alternatively, a computerised guidance system can be used and the AGV navigates by reference to an internal 'map' of its surroundings.

Quality. The accurate positioning on the pallet assures consistent set-up accuracy at each work station, while the consistent transfer process protects from transit damage and the possibility of losing parts.

Delivery. Although some flexibility of routing is possible, the need for AGVs is based on distributed process work stations. If the process flow paths could be brought closer together, materials handling may be simpler. In complex situations, the management of the AGV traffic becomes a problem and delivery may be adversely affected.

Cost. This is a capital intensive approach requiring significant continuing costs and may be justified to support unmanned operation or through the set-up reductions and quality aspects. It needs careful evaluation and some vision of a longer time horizon.

Advanced Manufacturing Technologies (AMTs)

This was defined by the UK government's Advisory Committee on Applied Research and Development as ''...... any substantial, relevant and new manufacturing technique which, when adopted, is likely to require a change not only in manufacturing practice but also in management systems and the manufacturer's approach to design and production engineering of the product."

Automated Storage and Retrieval Systems (AS/RS)

This is a system of computer-controlled stores and material handling and location systems. It provides high density storage in an efficient manner and relatively rapid recovery of stored material. It was regarded as the way forward in manufacturing before we all began to question why we need stocks of material. It can still have a role to play in tool storage and perhaps for particular distribution-related approaches (perhaps for reasons of product support after the normal production life has terminated).

Quality. It minimises damage in transit through careful storage design methods and by avoiding incorrect issues of material would avoid faulty product assembly.

Delivery. For normal manufacture such a quantity of parts would tend to suggest long lead times and slow response. This does not contribute to effective manufacture. For very long lead time parts which cannot be shipped into the factory on an 'as required' mode, the AS/RS could be used to control the flow of material into the plant on a trickle basis.

Cost. This is a capital intensive approach for large quantities of material. As such, it may well have an adverse effect on cost performance.

Automated Test Equipment (ATE)

This is often applied to electronic equipment which has to be tested as a functioning system, as well as earlier tests of components. It operates under computer control to cycle through a battery of test situations and provide information about quality performance.

Quality. The major reason for use, for the complex product, is indispensable.

Delivery. This is the rate of throughput often determined by the equipment. Strategies for re-test and repair affect delivery performance. Flexibility will be affected by the ease of re-programming, and perhaps fixturing, to pick up the correct test points.

Cost. It can be expensive and requires high technical support staff, but quality savings should outweigh.

Computer Aided Design (CAD)

CAD is a computer hardware and software combination to provide significant assistance to design visualisation, calculation and drawn output. Essentially it creates a computer model of a physical entity which can be stressed, modified, dynamically simulated and dimensioned to ensure proper fit between mating parts. The computerised model can provide the base data for much downstream activity in production and inventory control and in costing. It provides tools to manage the introduction of new products by control of the engineering changes.

Quality. A major impact by making it easier for designers to try alternative solutions, to design quality and reliability into the product at source, as well as permitting more effective design for production. By using the same data, transcription errors are minimised.

Delivery. Particularly for designs having some similarity to existing ones, CAD can significantly reduce the lead time for the technical development of new product. There is a major reduction in the time to make design changes and re-draft drawings, and the provision of basic product data reduces time along the manufacturing path.

Cost. There is a wide price range of available systems, but this is justified by total system benefits rather than by productivity improvements of designers, since much of design time may well be thinking time rather than data input at the computer. Product cost reductions are possible through better design, and better design practice can be forced by making it easier for designers to choose standard components, rather than re-inventing the wheel. CAD can also produce parts lists automatically, thereby reducing errors through misunderstanding. Finally, digitised product definition data and process instructions facilitate shopfloor automation.

Computer Aided Engineering (CAE)

CAE can be used interchangeably with CIM (see later), but more often is regarded as the whole area of CAD/CAM, including CNC/DNC and CAPP (see later). For the effects on the deliverables, see the individual entries.

Computer Aided Manufacture (CAM)

This is usually taken to refer to the automatic control of a manufacturing process, such that a complete definition of the means to produce a part has been established down to the tools and tool paths to be taken and all operations calculated and listed. CAM works from the geometry specified and digitised at CAD to provide the control instructions for manufacture and inspection processes.

Quality. Assuming the control instructions have been properly generated, the consistency of production is improved. The calculations of tool paths often requires computer assistance to reduce the effort and risks of errors in tedious calculations. There has been a tendency to see this as a task for planners separate from the machine operators, but some machines provide for data input at the machine, so that a skilled operator can have his skill developed, rather than replaced by the machine. Machines controlled in this way are inherently more consistent than manually operated ones.

Delivery. For given part requirements, the change-over time is much reduced. For completely new products, the generation of the toolpath instructions can create a new queuing problem to pass through the off-line planning function.

Cost. Some reduction in shop floor operator costs may be possible, but new planner skills can be more expensive. The quality argument should be enough to justify.

Computer Aided Process Planning (CAPP)

Process planning establishes the means and machines of production and historically has been performed by industrial or production engineers. Computer aids aim to take the CAD data and automatically generate the manufacturing instructions. This approach is likely to require some form of knowledge based system to capture the experience of the engineers and build that into the computer program suite.

Quality. Automation should remove human variability from process planning and make repeatable, standard plans quickly, which can be chosen to provide quality output.

Delivery. In a high product variety situation, CAPP may reduce lead time significantly; in low variety standard product business, it is unlikely to be a high priority.

Cost. Benefits would come through the above, but as yet there are few systems to choose from.

Computer Integrated Manufacturing (CIM)

This is seen as the long-term future for many companies. It is the complete operation of the business, utilising all the developed technologies and approaches, often employing hierarchies of computer systems operating from shared data in central or distributed databases. In theory, this would be the 'lights out' automatic factory of the future. Major difficulties remain to interface different kinds of manufacturers' equipment to enable the integration process to take place. Such a total system would have developed links to the outside world through other computer systems and can be envisaged in a science fiction manner as 'black box manufacture', with a demand going in at one end and a completed product coming out the other to satisfy that demand. By definition, quality and delivery would be good in such a system, but the cost of the complexity may make the cost benefit difficult to establish. CIM is more a philosophy than a technology, but is predicated on removing people from manufacturing – but often the people costs are not that important.

Coordinate Measuring Machines (CMMs)

These take the same data generated by the CAD system to operate inspection machines for crucial quality features. Their use can be as normal inspection machines to sanction an approval for onward transmission of parts to the next processing stage, or to customers. Their rate of inspection can approach the throughput time of the processing equipment and, as such, it can be more economic to consider 100% inspection of outgoing goods, but it must be realised that inspection after manufacture is added time and cost and can be considered as waste. If it is possible to so control the process of production as it happens that rejects do not occur, there may still be a role for CMMs to monitor drift in process capability and gain even better control over the process.

Quality. This is the main function of this type of equipment and operates as a very effective filter to remove bad quality from the flow of product, as well as providing trend data for analysis and improvement activity.

Delivery. CMMs will improve lead times to the extent that inspection becomes a normal shop-floor activity, thereby avoiding the need for separate, strictly controlled inspection areas manned by quality personnel, where new queues can form to delay progress. In the limit, however, inspection adds time and, if the necessity for it can be removed, then lead times will improve.

Cost. The use of CMMs is a capital intensive approach which may be justified for complex product geometries in high value parts. In such cases the quality and delivery improvements could be significant.

Computer Numeric Control/Direct Numeric Control (CNC/DNC)

Numeric control is the process by which control instructions are communicated to a machine tool to control its speed of operation and feed-rate of tool, as well as the relative position of the tool to the material surface. NC operates by coding the instructions on a punched paper tape, which has to be mounted into the processing equipment and read by the machine. CNC avoids the paper tape and uses computer means to aid the generation of the coded instructions. DNC takes the exercise a stage further by a central computer holding the coded programs for a number of machines and their associated parts in store until required. Downloading of these part programs is decided by the DNC controller, which is thus able to control a cell of machines.

Quality. It is possible to define optimum processing approaches in the part program, thereby thinking quality in at that stage. Thereafter the programs will repeat each time they are properly loaded, so consistency of output is also much improved. The process of numerical control replaces the motor skills of the machine operator by the analytical skills of the part programmer (who could be the same person suitably re-trained). By removing the human element from the machine control system, we remove human variability, and this explains the increase in repeatability.

Delivery. Machine change-over times are much reduced with these methods. Tooling changes might also be under DNC control, perhaps with in-built tool magazines at the machine. Failing this, tooling changes are likely to be the longest aspect of the change-over time, since the time to change the program can be negligible under DNC and short under the others. Physical set-up time will depend on whether standard work holding fixtures are being used. If they are, they will have been set to a datum point which the machine's program will seek out and then use as the reference point for the movements thereafter.

Cost. The quality and delivery improvements are likely to be so significant that higher initial capital cost becomes less important. The changing skill argument is an important one to recognise, particularly if the investment appraisal approach is overly attentive to possible direct labour cost reductions.

Flexible Manufacturing Centre, Cell or System (FMC/FMS)

A machining centre is a machine tool capable of doing a variety of the tasks associated with a number of separate machines, without the necessity to remove the part from the machine, thereby removing the waste of multiple set-ups. Thus a lathe may have, in addition to a variety of turning tools, perhaps a driven tool in its system capable of performing some milling operations. Gauging sensors can also be in-built to reduce losses in that direction. A cell adds more than one machine, or centre, to a given location. Now we need to control material movement around the cell, or from machine to machine. The system puts more of these elements together under central computer control. Material transfer can become more of a problem requiring the use of AGVs to coordinate the feeding and re-tooling of the machines.

In all of these approaches the word flexible appears, but there are a number of different types of flexibility, including those actually achieved as opposed to those hoped for. Many existing FMSs are a lot less flexible than the use of the word would imply and great care is required to correctly specify the precise need for flexibility in the market place before designing the system, for it is likely to be a very expensive solution to a business need.

Quality. Improvements come from the CNC/DNC machines in the system and the control over material handling.

Delivery. One of the stated aims of FMSs is to move towards an economic batch of one. Certainly the processing batches tend to be much smaller, thus improving delivery performance. Such high levels of automation also provide opportunities to improve delivery, by running more continuously and perhaps unmanned at unsocial times.

Cost. If it can truly be made economic to produce in small quantities, then costs reduce. One attractive way of utilising the flexibility of such systems is to produce matched sets of combining parts for later assembly. Producing in this way could greatly reduce stock holdings.

Programmable Logic Controllers (PLCs)

These are used to control pieces of equipment which are required to operate in a fixed sequence, or on receipt of relayed signals. They have tended to be inflexible, but by having the controls in software rather than hard-wired, as before, we can permit more variety in control sequences and the PLCs begin to look more like NC variants.

Quality. Consistency is the watchword here and quality variations become less.

Delivery. Until software controls these would not have greatly aided delivery, but the speed of change now helps considerably.

Cost. PLCs have relatively low cost entry into automation and, if re-programmable, can provide flexibility-related cost reductions.

Robotics

In the West the definition of a robot tends to emphasise the easily re-programmable nature of the more sophisticated material and tool handling manipulators used in a variety of processing operations and in some (fewer) assembly ones. The Japanese definition tends to include much simpler pieces of equipment of the 'pick and place' type, but, even allowing for that, there is a much higher number of robots installed in Japanese industry than anywhere else.

Robots have had their major impact in activities that are unpleasant or difficult for human workers. Paint spraying and spot welding of car bodies are examples of this. Robots bring consistency of operation once 'taught' the correct sequence and movement paths and can operate continuously (sometimes without a product being present). Robotic assistance is being applied to machine tools to aid change-overs and robotic assistance in packaging can be useful. Assembly is proving to be more difficult, due to the prior dependence on the inherent flexibility of human workers. Thus, a part that arrives in slightly the wrong position poses no problem to the visually coordinated person, but can cause a robot to fail. In similar fashion, a part which is less than perfectly designed for assembly can be manipulated by the dexterous human to produce the product.

Attempts to get round this problem tend to follow two directions. The first tries to make the robot essentially more life-like in providing vision systems to recognise mis-fed parts and compliance and feel to correct for fit problems. The alternative approach is to so design the parts that they can only be assembled correctly and design the assembly system so that faulty orientation is corrected prior to causing an assembly problem. The interesting feature of this latter approach is that, by such design effort, the task is made so simple that human assemblers can often at least match the robot in throughput while still retaining the inherent flexibility which has to be engineered into the robot system.

Quality. In many cases the experience of a skilled person can be captured by the robot system and so quality performance can be transferred and repeated every time the sequence of actions is run. In other cases the sheer controllability of the robot movements means that levels of quality are improved. An example would be in the welding of a complicated geometry path, where a human would have difficulty manoeuvring the welding torch and at the same time keeping all the physical relationships constant.

Delivery. Robotic systems have made great improvements in the ability of production systems to accept changes in requirement at an acceptable change-over cost and time.

Cost. Increased flexibility can reduce the capital cost of hardware through avoiding the need for additional equipment, thereby reducing manufacturing cost. Quality improvements are beneficial in themselves.

At this point we will halt our consideration of the hardware based AMTs. As mentioned before, we have not discussed particular processing technologies, or made any reference to new materials technologies, which might require novel ways of processing. It is to be expected that such innovations will be justified, either on product market criteria and/or on grounds of process improvement, in which case the quality, delivery and cost arguments will need to be evaluated.

SOFTWARE-BASED APPROACHES

Electronic Data Interchange (EDI)

This refers to approaches to communication between companies which is organised along data pathways rather than by paper-based systems. These data pathways can be exclusively dedicated to the particular link, but more realistically would be most appropriate where a group of companies can communicate through some form of network system capable of handling textual, numerical and graphical information. A variety of such *value added networks* are becoming available, often related to particular market sectors, like retail, automotive, aerospace and electronics.

The actual purpose of the data transmission provides some additional complications. If all that is being communicated are call-off order quantities from a customer to its supplier, then a relatively simple system will suffice. If, on the other hand, a supplier wishes to interrogate his customer's database of forward orders to see how the demand pattern is changing in order to better plan his own response, then we are into other considerations.

Not only do we need the communication link between both parties, but we need to have sufficiently compatible computer systems at both ends, such that the enquiry of one database produces information in a form understandable by the computer system at the other end. This becomes even more difficult when we consider transmitting design data from company to company, or even between distributed parts of the same organisation if they were previously allowed a free reign in computer purchases.

The data generated from a CAD system would be very valuable to a supplier company at an early stage in the design process. Such data could be examined to establish the ease of manufacture by the supplier, who might be able to suggest improvements based on their specialised knowledge of their technology. A two-way flow of design ideas depends even more on the standard ways in which the geometric data is represented and stored in the CAD system, and, until much better standards are developed and agreed, the difficulties are so great the major buyers are putting pressure on their suppliers to think very seriously before purchasing a CAD system different from their own. Of course, the supplier may have a number of major customers each with their own systems and life gets complicated. Major efforts are underway to resolve some of the standardisation problems, but, until this is complete, the total benefits will be hard to achieve.

Quality. The main benefit comes from the potentially collaborative efforts in design, where a variety of experts can quickly have an input at the design thought processes and easily try out alternatives, for cost as well as function. Quality can also be improved by avoiding transcription errors inherent in paper systems. Conversely, security needs to be well managed to avoid accidental or malicious damage by freer access to computer systems. In theory, better information availability would allow more informed decision-making, but people must be better trained to understand the implications of decisions made locally for data stored remotely and used in a variety of other ways by others in other organisations with whom they may never be in contact.

Delivery. This has the potential to provide a very significant reduction in the total manufacturing leadtime, both at the design end of the range and during a part supply operation. Weeks can easily be cut from the design lead-time, while part supply can be measured in hours for geographically close suppliers. Such improved responsiveness provides the opportunity to offer increased product ranges and modifications to the market place in an effective and controlled manner.

Cost. By replacing inventory and time by information flow, some costs increase, but the likelihood is that overall cost will reduce. It remains a high cost investment currently, but it is hard to find a reason to doubt its continued development.

Group Technology (GT)

This recognises the fact that even in a situation where product variety is wide, there can often be a high degree of similarity in the components which go to make up the product. Thus, it may not be possible to lay out the factory to gain the benefits of flow-line production for a particular product, but by identifying the families of similar components a form of mini mass production system can be set up to manufacture efficiently this group of components.

A group technology cell will thus be set-up with sufficient processes included within it to avoid the need to transport materials from one location to another – simply to enable another process operation to be performed. Such cells will often have more machines than people, who therefore have to be capable of operating a variety of machines as and when the pattern of work demands.

The family of components can be found by geometric similarities, by dint of their needing similar process operations, or by the similarity in their requirement for tooling. One of the immediate benefits is to reduce the costs of setting-up tooling for the component variety, since this can be designed into the normal pattern for the cell. The geographic proximity of plant tends to be close in such cells, thereby permitting simple material handling approaches. Such cells can make for simplified production planning and control and can encourage more localised maintenance, quality control and decision making. In many ways GT is an enabling technology for FMS, but can show benefits on its own.

Quality. Improvements come from reduced material handling, controlled set-ups and worker identification with the family of parts and their requirements.

Delivery. Delivery can be much improved by virtue of the ability to handle very small batch quantities, since they fit easily into the family and can easily be processed alongside other demands. Transportation distances will be small and little time is lost in setting-up for new batch runs, so lead-time can be small.

Cost. Some cost is incurred in identifying the families initially and in ensuring that designers work within the established families where possible. Some additional equipment will probably be needed, and probably not be fully utilised, in order to control the flow of parts in the cell. However, the savings compared with traditional forms of plant organisation, largely through the inventory reductions possible, are likely to be substantial.

Just-in-Time (JIT)

This is not so much a technique as a philosophy of waste removal on a continuous path towards manufacturing excellence. It can be regarded as a 'catch all' for many of the new ways of thinking about the real role of manufacturing. JIT demands quality, ensures delivery and enables cost reductions.

One of the major wastes attacked by JIT is inventory, which is seen both to hide the underlying causes of problems and to create problems on its own. By removing inventory in an incremental fashion, problems can be exposed to critical scrutiny, a permanent solution applied, and the problem removed from consideration. The analogy is often drawn with a ship on a sea or river of inventory. As long as the level is high enough, the ship can float clear of dangerous rocks (i.e. the problems). Once inventory is reduced, however, the problem rocks come closer to the ship and may cause it to founder. This image is such a powerful one that we have tended to latch onto the inventory reduction possibilities without realising that the reduction in inventory is used by the Japanese as much to expose quality and delivery problems as to reduce inventory as an aim.

There is in JIT much that is simply good industrial engineering practice, but where the difference comes is in the attention to detail and the continuous striving for improvement. Fundamental to this process is the involvement of all of the company's people in this quest for improvement. In this way the real experts, i.e. the people who do the job, are encouraged to suggest ways of doing their job in a better way – one that improves the manufacturing deliverables and also makes their quality of work life better.

JIT brings together aspects still to be defined here, such as TQC/SPC, TPM and Pull Logistics, to produce a manufacturing system geared towards producing perfect quality just in time to satisfy a customer requirement with total reliability. The definition of customers is as we have used the term to recognise a supplier/customer relationship all the way along the supply chain, from raw material to final customer.

In order to be manageable, a company will tend to reduce the number of suppliers it deals with, but those that remain find themselves becoming much more integrated into the thinking of their customer with regard to new product design and development and forward planning.

JIT can be regarded as a philosophy to ensure the regular flow of material through the system to ultimate customers. In this sense it approaches the flow line ideals expressed in the development of 'Detroit style automation' which enabled Henry Ford to go from raw iron ore to finished Model T (any colour as long as it's black) in 33 hours. The Toyota version permits a wider variety of model types down the line and avoids the vertical integration of the Ford system. Note, however, that the financial structure of many of the larger Japanese companies often includes a shareholding in supplier companies. JIT thinking impacts all aspects of a company's activities and requires a high level of re-training and attitude modification in many companies.

JIT fits very nicely into the quality, delivery and cost improvement mould we have been building. Apart from the training costs, which in reality are not costs but investments in the human resource, JIT is not expensive to implement. In fact, releasing the inventory investment is usually enough to finance immediate costs, while the longer term benefits simply keep on building. Aspects of JIT do not fit every situation easily. It may be difficult for instance to remove stock totally from the system, because the demand variability is too great, and so buffers can be kept to insulate manufacturing to an extent. What is recognised, however, is the extent of the waste that such a policy creates and therefore a target for renewed effort at improvement at a more fundamental level.

Manufacturing Automation Protocol/Technical Office Protocol (MAP/TOP)

One major difficulty facing companies moving in the direction of more integration in its various business activities, is the problem of incompatible pieces of information technology equipment. This would not be a problem if it were possible to satisfy all requirements with one vendor's kit, but the practicalities are different. Companies even within the one location are likely to have a variety of suppliers of computer-related equipment, each with its own idiosyncrasies in terms of operating systems and communications methods. Thus, General Motors in factory automation and Boeing in design automation found that the existing standards were simply not well enough established to meet their needs. As a result, they began a user-led drive to set interim standards to permit interconnection of dissimilar equipment which would allow some progress to be made while the international standards committees deliberated on the 'best' pattern for the future. This must be a very short term problem, since in the longer term it will be necessary for there to be a standard form of data communication in the form of an information utility, so that it will be possible to plug into the information ring mains in the same way that a piece of electrical equipment plugs into the power supply mains.

Quality. The aim of both protocols is to ensure that data communications are not corrupted in transit from one machine to another. By definition, therefore, quality will be improved by avoiding these forms of error.

Delivery. Efficient communications would permit improvements in the speed of reaction of a business and must therefore be of major importance - once it is correct.

Cost. At the present time this will not save money. In fact the effort of moving fast in this direction is probably only feasible for the very large, technically sophisticated companies. Nevertheless, companies considering major new facilities would do well to consider how they should put a data utility infrastructure in place ready for the solution when it comes along. It is likely, for instance, that it will be easier to instal the fibre optic cable, or whatever, in a ring main system as the building is going up, rather than fitting it round everything once they are installed. In this scenario, information is a service like electricity, water or hydraulics, but not yet.

Material Requirements Planning/Manufacturing Resource Planning (MRP/MRPII)

MRP started as a result of the realisation that traditional methods of managing production based on stocking policies were simply not appropriate in situations where the demand for component items is calculable precisely from a knowledge of the demand for the product of which they are components. This is the case in batch manufacture, where once the demand for the finished product is known or decided, then there is a simple arithmetic relationship which creates the actual volume requirements for the component parts. This is done by interrogating the design database in the form of a 'bill of material' to establish in what sequence a product is manufactured and how many lower level items are required to produce the quantity of higher level items.

Manufacturing or procurement lead times are allowed for in determining when to action an order and so it becomes possible to foresee future loads on the manufacturing unit. MRP generally considered the production facility to have an infinite capacity. To get round this problem MRPII was developed. This offered some capability to examine whether there was in fact capacity available to meet the calculated production requirement. If not, the Master Production Schedule (MPS) could be amended following consultation with Marketing and the customer.

The MPS therefore became a major link between marketing and manufacture and provided a means actually to make promises that had a chance of being met because the existing commitments had been examined and were seen not to interfere with the desired plan. MRPII effectively closed the feedback loop from market plan through manufacturing capability back to the plan again. It could also be used in a 'what if' capacity to examine the future load on various resources, hence its new title. It also had the merit that the unit of planning and measure became the piece-part to which could be allocated cost information.

Thus, MRPII could be seen as a complete information system which could be used by financial controllers as well as production controllers, buyers and salesmen making delivery commitments. MRPII is, however, a highly complex suite of software programs requiring very high levels of data accuracy and therefore discipline from all users, since without these, chaos comes quickly.

Quality. There is nothing inherently quality-improving about MRPII, apart from the need for accurate data as a prerequisite. In some respects, MRPII can make it easier to accept poor quality, since it is easy to factor in an allowance for scrap into the quantity multiplier in the 'bill of material'. This can then become a norm, which might be left unchallenged. Batching of orders can still be used, thereby allowing quality defects not to be immediately recognised.

Delivery. MRPII has a powerful ability to manage delivery against the MPS but, unless actively managed, the assumed lead times build in time buffers, which increase the supply lead time. The capability to examine forward load does permit a statement of delivery to be made with some confidence, and for complex products being produced in variety it has much to offer. It is worth noting that, in theory, an MRP system has the capability to produce only as and when required, so approaching a JIT result. Note, however, that the principle of the MPS is to *push* orders into the system sometimes in anticipation of an actual customer order. If this does not in fact materialise, we have built inventory for which there is no immediate sale.

Cost. The requirement to ensure high levels of data accuracy and the cost of the hardware and software, not to mention the training effort, means that such systems are expensive to instal. The potential is there to generate cost savings by gaining control of the material flows in the plant, and reductions in inventory levels can be of the order of 20-30%. There would not, however, appear to be the same potential for continuous improvement that is seen in JIT.

Optimised Production Technology (OPT)

This is another highly computer dependent approach to the total management of a manufacturing operation. It works from new definitions of how to manage the production of complex products in relatively lower volumes than the JIT ideal, and can be seen as more obviously competitive with MRPII (although complimentary might be even better).

OPT challenges the accounting principles that many take for

granted. It defines *throughput* as material which can be immediately translated into money through sales, and therefore focuses on actual customer requirement in the same way as JIT. *Inventory* is any material which is in the process of being transformed into throughput, and *operating expense* is everything else.

The argument then goes that the objective is to make money and therefore to maximise throughput while simultaneously reducing inventory and operating expense. In order to do this, it becomes necessary to identify those *capacity restrained resources* or *bottlenecks* which can reduce the amount of throughput. OPT argues that there are relatively few such bottlenecks and manages the whole production system to ensure no loss of time at them. It works back from customer demand to the bottleneck, optimises throughput at the bottleneck, and then ensures that all other operations support the bottleneck. This can often mean creating time buffers of work waiting at the bottleneck, or on other paths leading to a merged operation with material from the bottleneck, but not elsewhere.

In fact, by this way of thinking the other operations do not need to be operating continuously and could easily be made to operate on small batch sizes to keep the flow through the bottleneck balanced. In order to find the bottlenecks a major analysis of the factory is needed and, in fact, can make use of an MRP database if one exists. Additional data is required, however, and the software that does the detailed scheduling is proprietary, so that many companies have taken the concepts of OPT and incorporated them into their own systems.

Quality. By highlighting the importance of the bottleneck operation, OPT points to the need to manage quality in the supply of material to and from the bottleneck. Its quality improvement efforts are probably more targeted than JIT and therefore perhaps not seen as such a global activity.

Delivery. The focus on throughput and customer requirement ensures a high level of customer satisfaction across a variety range and would seem to be worth it for that alone in some cases.

Cost. For complex products, often competing for scarce resources, there seems little doubt that savings can be dramatic, but then the installation cost can be too.

Preventive Maintenance (PM)

Maintenance activity can fall into two broad categories of *breakdown* and *preventive*. The first simply reacts to problems as and when they occur and tries to minimise the damage caused by the failure. In a system full of inventory, the buffers of material can permit downstream activities to continue for some time before any serious impact is felt. In a system which reduces inventory to much lower levels, there is much more potential disruption to the integrated production chain from a failure in one of its links.

For this reason it is important to forestall failure by instituting a procedure to monitor equipment and note when it begins to show signs of needing more detailed attention from technical support staff. This can then be scheduled into the working time as best fits normal operating requirements. This monitoring does not need to be done by a skilled technician, rather it is seen as the way in which an interested worker would try and ensure that his process continued to produce satisfactorily, so that the worker would not be responsible for interfering with other parts of the flow.

Monitoring is one aspect, but other more mundane activities are also important. Simple acts of cleaning, oiling and general tidiness and care can be made part of the worker's responsibilities.

Quality. By avoiding breakdowns, the parts which might be damaged as part of the breakdown are avoided, thus reducing scrap. Monitoring for out of acceptable operational limits in the machine can also be part of a control over quality performance and will aid quality in providing timely information.

Delivery. Preventive maintenance can be seen as an interference with the flow of material if an operation must be halted to make a modification. The trick is to try and do the maintenance outwith normal production time. Some companies work an 8 - 4 - 8 - 4 shift pattern, the 4-hour shifts being devoted to the larger items of preventive maintenance. This regularity can avoid problems during the production shifts themselves.

Cost. In some respects PM increases the apparent cost of maintenance, in that more attention is being paid in the hope that breakdowns will not occur. The thinking is precisely the same as in the cost of quality argument. In the longer term, a shift to prevention-based costs reduces the total cost, because it saves the difficult to quantify, but no less real, costs of failure.

Pull Logistics

MRP is criticised as a 'push' system, in that it assumes a certain demand is appropriate and 'pushes' orders into the manufacturing plant in the hope that what finally arrives at the dispatch bay is what the customers actually require at that time. Push operates at the input end of the transformation, but the JIT argument is that it is more sensible to gear your production to actual customer demand and let that drive your delivery system, rather than some, perhaps notional, master schedule.

To this end, Pull Logistics works from the output end of the system. A customer requirement is satisfied from a minimal stock point, which is itself a signal to replenish that stock point. Unless that signal is received, then the feeding operation is not permitted to produce, since this would create inventory in excess of customer requirement. The pull signal can then ripple down the supply chain, indicating the need to move material or activate a manufacturing, or even a purchase, instruction. In Toyota's original version, the card signal was called a *Kanban*, but, in fact, a large variety of signals can be used in a variety of ways.

Pull Logistics are a major part of JIT, but they could equally be applied in an MRP environment, since MRP is not good at the shop-floor scheduling activity. Thus, MRP could be used for planning purposes and Pull Logistics could implement actual production at the shop-floor.

Quality. The minimum batch sizes that go with pull logistics suggest that quality must be good to make the material flow correctly. The small batch sizes also show up problems more quickly and so pressure can be brought to bear to improve the situation.

Delivery. This is very good, but it should be recognised that pull logistics has been most readily applied where the variety of products is not high. Attempting to institute this approach in a situation of high variety and complex products might only introduce inventory of the wrong kind at the wrong time.

Cost. Inventory reductions usually mean that this is an approach which is worth pursuing. It is also of itself not expensive to institute, but we should note that it is really just the material control aspect of a much more integrative approach, which must also be properly implemented to allow for success in this aspect.

Statistical Process Control (SPC)

This was discussed in Chapter 1. It is built around the fact that any process subject to a wide variety of influences produces results that are not precisely what was intended, but which vary in a regular way which is recognised statistically as a *normal* distribution. Fig. 2 in Chapter 1 showed a normal distribution.

In SPC the normal distribution produced by a particular process, working on the kinds of products we are currently producing, is used to monitor whether anything unusual is happening to cause the process to produce a changed shape or location of the distribution. For example, a drill cutting holes in metal will produce slightly different sizes of hole because of vibrations, temperature fluctuations, human setting variability, etc. As the drill loses its sharpness, the diameter of the drill will reduce slightly. The result is possibly the same variation in sizes, but on average the holes will be slightly smaller. Only if something changes in some fundamental way will the overall shape of the distribution change. Nevertheless, we must control for both situations.

Fig. 4 shows a statistical control chart for the average of a particular measurement. This is calculated from trial runs to establish the distribution location and shape. Once the shape can be drawn, we can make use of other aspects of statistics to recognise that only some 2.5% of the distribution lies at a distance of 2 standard deviations from the average value. (N.B. Standard deviation is a measure which describes the distribution's shape according to how widely or closely spread are the values under consideration.)

By taking small samples from our process at regular intervals and measuring their average size and plotting the results onto a chart, we can build up a picture of trends developing over time. As long as the averages of the samples lie within the $+/-2$ standard deviation limits, then we can be fairly sure that the process is still in statistical control. If we get a result at A in

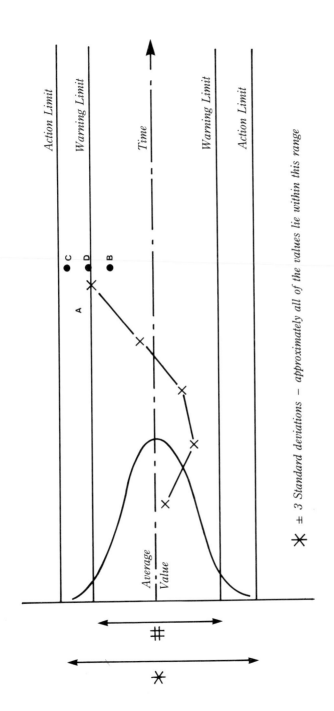

Fig. 4 Statistical control chart for sample averages

✱ ± 3 Standard deviations – approximately all of the values lie within this range

\# ± 2 Standard deviations – approximately 95% of all values lie within this range

Fig. 4, there is a probability that we are still in control, but we are now suspicious that the process is changing in some fundamental way. Additional samples will be taken and the results plotted.

A result at B would indicate that control is still all right and that the previous result was due to chance. The process could then continue with samples being taken at the previous frequency. A result at C, or even D, suggests that the location of the average value has moved (upwards in this diagram) and that the process cannot be considered to be in statistical control. (Please remember, however, that it is the relationship between the distribution shape and the design specified tolerance band which will define if reject material is actually produced.) Such results would suggest that we re-set the process to bring it back into control. Notice that we can be wrong in our interpretation, but we know the probability of that error.

Of course, we must also control for the shape of the distribution and can do this in a similar fashion. As is fairly obvious, it is the inherent variability of processes which creates the concern for control, and one of the long term goals of a quality system should be to reduce the level of variability in all of the processes. SPC can be a useful tool in the meantime and can provide an indicator of how well we are doing. Of course, there may be limitations on resources to tackle the problems. One way round this is to make more resources available through training the process operators and their supervisors in the techniques of statistical control.

This is what the Japanese have been doing very well for almost three decades now and what major Western companies are now beginning to do on a much wider scale. The other, complimentary, thing is to target the control activities at those activities most likely to cause a quality problem. *Failure mode and effect* analysis is known in design reliability exercises to establish a causal chain between how a process can fail, what factors influence that failure, and how the failure is manifested in practice. This same thinking can be applied in all aspects of productive operation and key factors identified, which must be controlled to ensure high quality output. These key factors will then be the target for SPC actions.

Quality. SPC has an important role to play in an integrated approach to quality improvement. It is not sufficient of itself to guarantee success.

Delivery. It has little direct impact, except as a means to reduce failure which would interrupt the flow of materials. There may be a concern that by giving more responsibility to the process operators to do the sample inspections and control chart updating, this would interfere with their throughput performance, but, by designing the work in a satisfactory manner, this work can often be undertaken at times when the operator would otherwise be waiting for the machine to finish its operational cycle. The benefits of employee involvement in the effort of control over his/her process, suggest that any slight loss will be more than made up by improvements through the consistency of material flow. If the process is in fact a bottleneck, then it may still be appropriate for others to take the responsibility to manage the data collection and interpretation to ensure maximum throughput at the bottleneck.

Cost. There is undoubtedly a training cost incurred in introducing SPC widely in an organisation. Western companies have traditionally not recruited the level of worker who would normally take readily to statistical methods. Even engineering degree courses will spend vast amounts of time on applied mathematics and relatively little on statistics. This, again, is a cost that falls into the prevention category and should be regarded as an investment in the skills of the work people which will pay dividends in reducing the levels of quality cost overall.

Total Quality Control (TQC)

This suggests an all embracing role for quality in an organisation and some companies call their approach *company wide quality*. It works from the principle that quality really is everyone's business and that the total business system has to be so designed and managed to make it possible both to measure properly the true cost of quality and to identify where progress is too slow. It makes it part of every person's job to deliver a quality product to their customer, both internal and external. The aim is to so engineer all of the processes that it is actually easier to produce correct quality rather than to fail and not bother. When working well, it impacts obviously on quality and delivery as well as cost, so is an absolute prerequisite for any moves towards increased competitiveness. There is, however, no defined end point, since the goal is forever slightly out of reach. The effort to progress along the road is well worthwhile, however, but in terms of motivation probably needs regular influxes of new faces and new ideas to keep the momentum going.

World Class Manufacturing (WCM)

This is a concept coined by Richard Schonberger to indicate what a truly world class competitive manufacturing operation would be like. It is based on a number of the features discussed here, like TQC, PM, JIT and *employee involvement*. Schonberger's message seems to have struck a receptive chord in many managers and there is certainly much to think about in his books. He has been instrumental in causing a reappraisal of the ways in which we think about manufacturing. He does seem to suggest, however, that the solution will be universal and that, by releasing workers' creativity at the workplace, then problems will be solved.

Certainly there are reported some significant improvements from many different countries and industries. The author has still to be convinced that solutions will be identical and is more inclined to the view that the business context and environment will create their own influence on the appropriateness of a given solution. That some of the thought processes will be common, that some of the guiding principles will be the same, the author has little doubt, but each company is in some way different and each marketplace will have its own requirements which may argue for more tailored solutions. It therefore becomes a major task for senior management to set the manufacturing activity in its proper strategic role and this we will discuss in the next chapter.

SUMMARY

Rather than try and encapsulate a long chapter into more text, this summary tabulates the contribution made by the AMTs discussed.

In the table, major positive influences on the *manufacturing deliverables* are indicated by + + +, a noticeable impact by + + and minor by +. This covers *quality, delivery* and *cost* improvement. As a separate evaluation the relative cost of installing the particular AMT is also indicated but using $- - -$ to indicate an extremely costly investment requirement and grading down as before. This exercise is of course subjective, but why change now?

AMT	QUALITY	DELIVERY	COST	
			Improvement	Installation
Hardware-based				
AGVs	+	+	+	− − −
AS/RS	+ +	+	−	− − −
ATE	+ + +	+ +	+ +	− −
CAD	+ + +	+ + +	+ + +	− −
CAM	+ + +	+ + +	+ + +	− −
CAPP	+ + +	+ +	+	−
CMMs	+ +	+ +	+	− −
CNC	+ + +	+ + +	+ + +	−
FMS	+	+ +	+ + +	− − −
PLCs	+ +	+ +	+ +	−
Robotics	+ + +	+ + +	+ + +	− −
Software-based				
EDI	+ + +	+ + +	+ + +	− −
GT	+ +	+ + +	+ +	− −
JIT	+ + +	+ + +	+ + +	
MAP/TOP	+	+ +	+	− − −
MRP/MRPII		+	+	− − −
OPT	+ +	+ + +	+ + +	− − −
Pull Logistics	+ +	+ + +	+ + +	−
PM	+ +	+ +	+ +	− −
SPC	+ + +	+ +	+ + +	− −
TQC	+ + +	+ + +	+ + +	− −
WCM	+ + +	+ + +	+ + +	− −

4 STRATEGY

In this chapter we will examine the nature of strategy and how manufacturing can help or hinder the wider efforts of the company to gain success in the marketplace. In particular we will try to satisfy the following objectives:

- Recognise the importance of *strategy* to the success of the business.

- Understand the importance of competitive advantage and how this will define the order-winning criteria that manufacturing must help provide.

- Consider the decisions on structure and infrastructure which *underlie* the manufacturing strategy.

- Recognise that many AMTs provide more choices for managers in designing the system.

STRATEGY AND COMPETITIVE ADVANTAGE

The origin of the word strategy tells us much about how we should think about using it. In early days it described 'the Generals Art' and this militaristic influence is very appropriate. In war the object of the exercise is to defeat your opponent at minimum cost to your own side. In order to accomplish this all sorts of short-term tactical moves and longer term strategies can be employed. Not all of these will necessarily be expected to succeed, rather they can be seen as required to prepare the enemy in some way to drop his guard in time for the final drive for victory.

Business success is in some ways similar to war. In business even more than in war, there is little likelihood of a final solution to the conflict. Battles can be won but in the medium term the adversary is likely to return to the fray, usually with some new development designed to swing the balance more in his favour. In the longer term, countries appear to have a cycle of success in general terms and then to become less competitive overall. The successful companies on a global scale manage in some way to transcend the tendency to decline and often become less dependent on their home base roots as they move to a multinational capability.

The conflict that is business has relative success and failure interchanging dynamically

The two main lessons to be drawn so far are that strategy is both competitive and dynamic. We will return to competitive issues later but for the moment let us concentrate on the fact that the situation is not static.

This fact is amply demonstrated in any competitive market where what was good enough for success yesterday is still necessary but no longer sufficient today. Thus there must be a conscious effort applied to identify what is needed or is likely to be needed for success in the new situation.

Strategy is also about recognising that resources cannot have the same impact if spread evenly around the the whole area of competitive struggle. Just as the general seeks to identify the enemy's weak spot and then throws his own strength against there in an attempt to break through, so must a business continually monitor the situation to prepare defences and gather its forces for the next onslaught.

What wins battles is not always the same thing every time

In the military, what wins battles is not always the same thing every time. On one occasion superior training and motivation of the fighting force overcomes the odds. Another time it may be the nature of the equipment used that creates the advantage, while another time sheer luck turns the tables in a totally unforeseen fashion. Often the nature of the logistics supply lines creates or destroys advantage. In similar fashion we must be careful not to expect that there is an easy solution to the competitive struggle in manufacturing business. In fact it may well be one of the features of the Western business world that we are too easily persuaded of the merits of a particular 'solution' and as a result assume that nothing else remains to be done. In this way companies move from one 'panacea' to another as new 'flavours of the month' are pushed by the latest guru. In fact, if JIT were more obviously technique rather than philosophy driven, there would be a worry that it would follow the same path to discreditation as others before it.

It follows from the dynamic nature of strategy that when we define the manufacturing portion of that strategy then we must do it in the expectation that as the strategy changes then so must the translation of that into the requirements of manufacturing. *Timescales to effect change are not uniform across organisational areas* Of course it must also be recognised that the timescales to effect change are not uniform across a single business and so due allowance must be taken of the ability to respond to such changes – in fact such an ability may well be a source of advantage in the struggle against the competition.

Strategy is obviously goal-directed and is concerned with the overall allocation of resources. Lower level plans and action programmes put the strategy into effect and so a hierarchy of strategic, tactical and operational planning takes place. Fig. 5 shows in outline form the nature of the process, but before examining that in more detail let us consider the centrality of the concept of *competitive advantage*.

The purpose of any strategic evaluation of a business is to identify that one or few major factors which positively discriminate in favour of your business seen from the perspective of your customers who after all are the final arbiters of success or failure. *Competitive advantage is that feature (or those features) that you supply in a fashion which your competitors cannot immediately compete with* The competitive advantage is that feature or features which you supply in a fashion which your competitors cannot immediately compete with. It could be any combination of the various items which go to make up the mix of things which constitute the *product,* the *delivery system* and the *cost.*

The difference from the manufacturing deliverables is simply one of emphasis. From the customer viewpoint, the product is the core, and quality one of its very important components. We can subdivide each of these into their constituent parts as shown below:

- *Product*   Capability – need satisfaction, state of the art.

    Performance – function, quality and reliability, aesthetics, ergonomics.

    Features – variety, customisation.

- *Delivery*   Availability – timeliness, location, packaging.

    Performance – lead time, reliability, transport.

    Features – quantity.

- *Cost*   Purchase price.

    Life cycle cost/ownership cost.

    Value for money.

    Non-price value features.

Any business can decide to operate a different mix of these various factors and to change them as a result of evaluation from the marketplace as to customer and competitor reaction. Given that it is a competitive situation, the best kind of advantage comes from something which can be protected from the copying attempts of the competition. This is always going to be a limited advantage since there are few factors which cannot be replicated given the time and resources. Even patents provide only limited protection in many cases and the wise company recognises this and aims to make best use of the temporary advantage before moving on to a new definition of advantage.

Some of the more enduring factors often turn out to be those dependent on human relationships either in providing the product or in the customer/supplier relationship. Given good results in this area, customers may be willing to allow a supplier time to react to a competitor's new advantage before they make a decision to switch companies.

Competing on cost needs careful examination – it is often self-defeating

One of the worst features on which to compete is price where, if no other consideration is present, a competitive battle will only result in diminishing returns to both competitors if the marketplace is limited in numbers. Of course, if by lowering prices more customers can be found, then the company best able to survive on lower margins may well win a major victory.

Each choice is likely to have its risks and countervailing forces, so the establishment of the strategy is the most important activity for the senior management of the company.

Fig. 5 shows in outline the process of strategy consideration in a manufacturing company but requires some further elaboration.

We have already indicated the crucial role of the top level decision maker(s) in setting the broad parameters for the future of the business. In many British and American companies this group has often not included a strong representation from the manufacturing arm of the company, rather favouring financial and marketing specialists. This would be less of a problem were we not also to train our managers in relatively narrow specialised functions. When this happens it is not surprising if a chosen strategy places unrealistic demands on the manufacturers. They are of course not blameless however, since they have not developed a language or conceptual structure to communicate the essence of manufacturing in a form that general managers from other disciplines can understand and empathise with. We should remember that our successful European and Japanese competitors do not have this problem since many of them will have wide experience of many different activities within the company and will frequently also be technically qualified to understand the technical decisions involved both in product design and manufacture.

A narrow educational and career pattern can make it difficult for senior managers to understand the wider systems view

The corporate decision maker(s) will have a view of the current situation as to its degree of acceptability and an opinion as to what the likely pattern of future scenarios might be given certain assumed actions by this and other companies, governments, etc. The element of future 'vision' must be informed by extensive inputs from environmental scanning, market research, technological forecasting, political, social and economic briefings from all areas of the world which currently or potentially impact the business activities of the company.

These views may be influenced by the business philosophy of the company. Such a philosophy might be to be the technological leader in a particular field, to build a business based on concern for customers, employees and shareholders, or to be consistently successful financially regardless of the actual

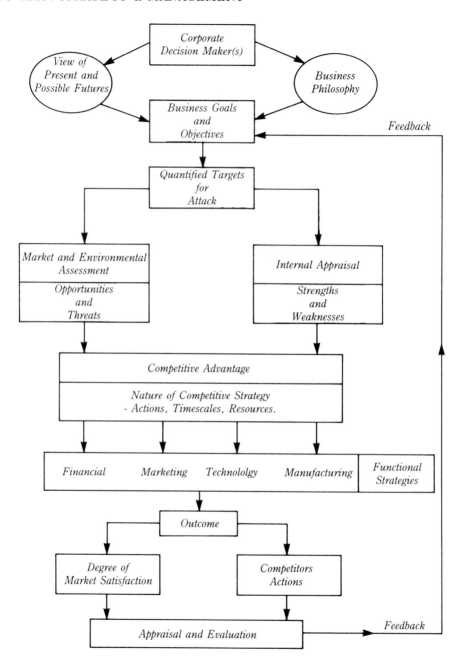

Fig. 5 Strategy formulation

area of activity.

This can be translated into broad business goals and objectives. The more general statements of intent being the goals and quantified targets being the objectives against which performance can be measured. It is worth noting that companies often have tendencies not to follow every path which opens for them. Companies will tend to follow particular technologies (e.g. electronics, mechanical engineering, polymer processing) or to stay in certain markets (e.g. healthcare, domestic appliances), or the truly diversified which follows any trend that promises good financial rewards. The significance of this is that, when present, such tendencies preclude accepting market opportunities outwith their immediate area of experience, expertise and comfort. There are good reasons for 'sticking to the knitting' but equally it must be recognised that such patterns limit the effective range of strategies open to the company and it is therefore important that lower levels in the organisation understand what is acceptable as well as potentially viable.

Companies often choose not to follow up recognised market opportunities

Should an opportunity appear which, although outwith normal activity, is sufficiently attractive, it may be possible to set up a small subsidiary operation to try it out commercially. If successful, the offshoot could always be floated off as an independent company.

Each of the foregoing considerations impacts on the quantified targets chosen to form the major strategic thrust for the next period. These will often be stated in terms of financial ratio measures of the 'return on capital employed' type or of percentage *market* share or rate of new product introduction or new market sector entered.

In order to identify precisely what must be done by the company to achieve these targets, a critical appraisal is needed of the particular market and general environmental situation in terms of the *opportunities* and *threats* posed, against the internal *strengths* and *weaknesses* demonstrated by the company.

SWOT analysis

Opportunities can come from developing existing products or markets, or from generating new products, or from opening up new market areas for complete or partial product lines. The implications for manufacturing depend on a mix of considerations, but any increase in product or component variety tends to mean a more difficult task for manufacturing – certainly until some of the more sophisticated AMTs are fully developed.

Threats can come from a variety of sources over which the company can have little if any control, in most cases. The main threat is obviously from competitors – actual or potential. Actual competitors are probably easier to monitor whereas potential competitors, especially from another country, pose particular problems. Governments can have a major effect on the nature of business opportunity through their attitude to investment, employment, transfer pricing and by their management of economic and exchange rate policies. The general stability of a country is important because of the long timescales involved in some investment decisions. The 'climate' for business is much affected by legislation as well as worker attitude and industrial relations practice. A major consideration is the supply chain to support a manufacturing plant. Materials must be available for conversion, distribution has to be properly organised, and often the supporting infrastructure of trained people and service businesses must be in place before a particular new market opportunity can be attacked sensibly.

When performing the internal appraisal, great care is needed because often what was once a strength can often turn out to be a weakness as the world changes without sufficient recognition inside the company. Thus the existing expertise in one market area can be a strength to be developed but may make it more difficult to change to a new requirement. In similar vein, existing organisational structures and operational systems can work for or against change and might actually produce a form of organisational sclerosis. A changing technological requirement might render redundant or irrelevant the developed people skills which in normal conditions would have produced a significant advantage. Conversely people skills to cope with and welcome change actually produce continuing strength.

People who have skills in welcoming and coping with change can produce continuing organisational strength

Overlying all this the current financial structure and performance can be a strength or a weakness, as can company size. What can be a serious weakness is a financial approach which has not been modified to recognise changing business criteria. There is evidence to suggest that that is precisely what has been happening to many UK companies as their accounting systems still operate according to conventions laid down for financial reporting purposes many decades ago and which tend to reinforce a short-term view of business activity.

Out of this critical evaluation of *strengths, weaknesses, opportunities* and *threats* comes a realisation of where the *competitive advantage* may lie. As indicated earlier, this advantage should be sustainable for a period of time sufficient to gain benefit and to develop the next strategic thrust. The definition of the competitive advantage will specify the actions, timescales and resources needed to create and maintain this advantage and may well also indicate contingency actions in the event of aggressive countermeasures from the competition.

From this stage onwards we begin to look in more detail into the implications of this chosen path for each of the main areas of activity in the business and create *functional strategies*.

The definition of the competitive advantage guides the development of functional strategies

The *financial* strategy will largely be represented by decisions as to sources of funding, financial structure of the organisation, investment criteria to be used in appraisal, and procedures for generating the funds for project implementation.

Marketing strategy is one where there is a great deal of interaction normally with higher level strategy decisions and is often built around the four Ps of the *marketing mix*, i.e. *product, promotion, place* and *price*. The *product* decision is a fundamental one in which all of the company should be represented. The product also has a service dimension and this must also be carefully planned. *Promotion* falls within the remit of the marketing function and involves everything to ensure that customers are aware of the benefits to be obtained by purchasing from the company. *Place* recognises that the product has to be delivered in order to satisfy. Traditional companies would often see the physical distribution of finished items and the management of the downstream supply chain as part of marketing's operation, but in terms of flow of information and material it is only one aspect of that chain and the real benefit will come when the whole chain is properly managed. *Price* covers the simple concept of cost of purchase but in many markets the total cost of ownership over a longer period of time is becoming relevant, and suitable ways of controlling that and promoting any benefits are also needed.

Marketing's 4 P's

Of course there are many complicating factors involved in this area of activity including concepts of market segments, sectors, niches and the role of *market intelligence* to monitor the business environment and thereby provide much of the data on which the identification of critical advantage can be based, is central to a sensible strategic evaluation and planning process.

Technology strategy will often not be separated out of other considerations. Often the assumption will be made that in considering the product decision, technology will be adequately covered. Now, in fact, the creative use of technology throughout all of the business can often support if not actually create the competitive advantage.

R & D – leader or follower

The major areas for consideration include the size of the resource devoted to *research* and *development*. Some companies have decided to compete almost on this alone and have moved to a strategy of sub-contracting the majority of the standard manufactured items in their products. Along with the scale of the investment comes a decision as to the focus for that investment. The main effort could be directed at pure 'state of the art' research without a concrete goal in mind, but perhaps only the very large organisation can afford that kind of speculative investment. By targeting more directly the desired outcome, companies move into a development mode which can be directed at products, manufacturing processes or operational systems. Such developments will utilise at least some of the AMTs previously discussed.

Another decision in the technology strategy area is concerned with the choice as to whether the company is to be a *leader* or *follower* in the state of the art. A leader runs risks of failing but may create an advantage difficult to attack in the short term. A follower avoids the up-front risks of unproven technologies but must duplicate or develop 'me-too' products fast enough to take some of the custom generated by the leader.

Technological scanning is needed

In both situations it is necessary to have some form of technological scanning in place to gain an understanding of what is or might be feasible. This will involve monitoring patent activity in the world, monitoring programmes of research in universities, for example, and studying media reports of competitors actions. This becomes an input to the market and environmental assessment already discussed.

MANUFACTURING STRATEGY

Manufacturing strategy is only just behind technology strategy in terms of newness to management thinking. For many years those companies that seriously tried to perform strategic analysis and plan, tended to the view that within certain fairly wide boundaries a manufacturing system could produce anything that was required. To an extent this was true within the envelope of existing technology and size. What was not understood and often still is not properly comprehended is that the problems of manufacture are often created or compounded by the actions of other functional areas in ways which are not always easy to demonstrate or quantify. In some respects that was one of the early benefits from MRPII installations where the requirement to agree a master production schedule between marketing and manufacture was instrumental in demonstrating the interconnectedness of changing production requirements.

Very often it is the relative speed of reaction that creates the problem and many of the AMTs impact on that. The timescale for major changes is likely to remain more of a problem, since new production facilities take time to order, install and bring up to full production throughput.

There are two sets of decisions to be made when considering manufacturing strategy. These are the type of *process* and the supporting *infrastructure*. Process decisions will tend to fall into the extended timescale category, whereas infrastructure is more people- and systems-related where change might be considered to be easier but often turns out to be problematical because of resistance to change in the current employees.

Decisions on process and supporting infrastructure are needed

In terms of process choice, the AMTs are affecting the normal patterns of relationship between type of process and volume of demand. On an increasing scale of volume of demand, the pattern would usually be as follows. Very low volumes, where the material often moved to where assembly took place and the final, usually large product, was completed would tend to be produced in a *project* mode. Increasing quantity of demand, but still in small unit or batch sizes, would be produced either in a *functional* layout or perhaps in a GT cell (see Chapter 3).

The functional layout draws together all similar kinds of equipment and produces the variety of parts by varying the sequence of visits to the different functional areas needed to complete a particular product. As volumes continue to increase the batch size can go up dramatically and elements of *discrete line flow* can then be justified. This is based on the production, in volume, of standardised or modular parts and products on highly engineered, repetitive manufacturing lines. At the extreme end of this spectrum we have continuous products, like oil or chemicals, where the plant also tends to run continuously producing a small variety by adding or subtracting from a menu

Process choices – project, functional, GT, discrete or continuous line flow

of constituents.

Each of these process types has particular features which help it cope with the circumstances for which it was designed, but make it less easy to cope with new requirements. For example, traditional line flow systems were designed to minimise manufactured cost of product producing a very low unit cost. They did this in a manner that made it very difficult to accommodate product variety, often needing a new plant to be built to produce a new generation of product. To try then to meet a new marketing opportunity for special products to customer specification would mean major disruptions to the flow of material and consequently increased costs. This is perhaps an obvious example and few companies would try to do this as a strategy but, in the middle range of volume of demand scale, companies do try and produce with the same facilities a range of output which creates completely different kinds of demands on the manufacturing system. This tendency to try and be all things to all men has been the bane of manufacturing people for decades.

Many of the AMTs are breaking up the process stereotypes

Many of the AMTs are breaking up these old stereotypes. In automobile assembly, for example, the introduction of robotics has meant not only that the plant can handle new product introductions without major retooling exercises, but also that a variety of products within a family can be progressed down the same line in an effective and efficient manner. In fact many AMTs are based on attempts to gain the economic efficiency of high-volume production but in situations where the batch size is very close to, if not actually, one. We must recognise, however, that what determines the kind of process that should be put in place should not simply be what makes life easier for the manufacturing function but what system best supports the already identified competitive advantage.

Infrastructure decision areas – role of (and responsibility for) quality, production, planning and control, and organisation and skills of the people

The other half of the equation is the infrastructure which is put in place to make the process fully effective. Three main areas are relevant here: the role of *quality* and the responsibility for quality; the form of *production planning and control*; and the nature of the *organisation* and skills of the people employed. Here again, many of the AMTs are impacting on the infrastructure area by offering managements more choice in how they wish to organise, plan and control the manufacturing system. It is also obvious that decisions about infrastructure can impact on the ways in which the process should change. For example, a move to JIT has major implications for plant layout, equipment purchase, maintenance, etc.

In order to facilitate the decision making process in manufacturing strategy, it is necessary to translate the competitive advantage statement into a definition of what manufacturing has to be good at to support the desired *strategy*. In this way the predominance of the customer is guaranteed and the implications of manufacturing process and infrastructure decisions can be recognised by others in the company. Such a procedure is likely to have a number of iterations as various possibilities are tried, modified and finally agreed.

Terry Hill has contributed a lot to thinking in this area by drawing a distinction between *qualifying and order winning criteria* in a particular market.

Identify the qualifying and order-winning criteria in the market place

In certain markets some factors act in some ways as gatekeepers. This means that unless a company satisfies this particular criteria, it is not allowed through the gate and into the market. Such a feature on its own will not necessarily be enough to win an order in the market, since if there are others in that market they must also have passed this particular test to gain entry.

The other important thing is to identify those factors which allow a product to win orders in that market. It may be some aspect of the product itself, its mode of delivery, promotion, or whatever, but it distinguishes it positively from the competition's offering and makes the customer want to purchase it. In effect we are asking for a more precise definition of the competitive advantage in a form that will tell manufacturing what it must do to translate that competitive advantage into performance in the market.

Factors can also be potential order losers. For example, it could be the case that price is not the order winner but if the price became too far adrift from those of the competition, then there would be no chance of winning the order regardless of the other good things on offer.

There can be movement between categories. Over time, what was once an order winner can become a qualifier and someone will then try and establish a new order winner. The personal computer market is a nice example of this tendency where, for example, a large amount of memory once won orders – now it is a qualifier *and* the thrust has moved on to speed. Similarly, in automobiles, where once many accessories were additional features to entice buyers they can often now be regarded as qualifiers. This is also a nice example of the multiple dimensions of strategic impact. By bundling the options into the basic specification of the car, manufacturers created a more immediately costly product to produce in terms of part count but one which was at the same time more standardised and easier to produce in volume, which tends to reduce costs. In the meantime, a market advantage over the competition meant increased sales. In this way, those companies obtained benefit at both ends of the relationship.

Qualifiers can also become order winners by redefining the standard of performance. Technological sophistication of the product could fall into this category. In certain markets a high level of technological capability is expected and is therefore a qualifier, but gaining a lead in the technology still wins orders.

The company discussed earlier is in this situation. For a number of years they thought that all they had to provide was technically sophisticated product, but a market analysis told them different. Their customers were expecting shorter delivery times, reliable high quality and a flow of improving products over reducing timespans. Their competitive edge was therefore defined to be R & D based with frequent new product introductions. As a result, the manufacturing requirement was to ensure that the capability to change was built-in and that effort was devoted to supporting that competitive edge. Manufacturing's task became one of creating and managing a supply chain of sub-contractors who do all of the non-sensitive manufacture and assembly. In-house, all that remains are the major value-added operations in assembly and final system test.

At the start of this chapter we identified the fact that strategy is dynamic. The implication of that is that those order winners identified today will not always remain so. There is therefore a requirement for this responsible for agreeing the competitive

Recognise how market requirements will change

advantage also to specify the order winning criteria and how they forecast that they will change. Depending on the confidence the company has in such forecasts and the length of the timescale over which change is expected, the manufacturing strategy decisions may well change. Until manufacturing systems are completely flexible (which may well be impossible if we allow material changes as well), there will still be a tendency for trade-offs to affect the final choice.

In essence, the trade-off argument is that a system can be designed to do certain things well but in so deciding we also explicitly or implicitly decide to do other things less well. In strategic terms, if the things we have decided to do less well are in fact going to be order winners in a few years or months time, and in the meantime we have invested in facilities which are difficult to modify, then the newly identified competitive advantage will not be provided by our company.

In strategic decision making there therefore must be an iterative loop of requirement, response, modified requirement and agreement. For this to happen management teams must be in a position to understand the nature of the other person's situation and to empathise with it. Unfortunately not all companies provide the degree of cross-training and mixed-function experience to make this a natural situation. There is a requirement to educate managers to think more strategically and to consider the effects of decisions across the total company system in order to define tasks for each of the functional areas that support and complement one another.

Strategy formation should be a loop of requirement, response, modified requirement and agreement by a team which understands each other's viewpoint

It is recognised that the kind of information required to help specify the manufacturing task will sometimes be difficult if not impossible to obtain reliably but when this happens the positive thing to do is not to commit to a manufacturing strategy which is less flexible than it could be.

Flexibility is not always the right thing to aim for. In fact, for commodity type products, the stereotype mass production, low unit cost process may still be the solution, but the message is that assumptions which have served us well for many years must be challenged before we accept them as still valid.

Having established detailed strategies for each of the functional areas, these must then be further developed into operational plans and put into effect.

The process must not however end there until perhaps the next annual review. The actual outcomes must be monitored, the degree to which we are actually satisfying the customer requirement measured, competitors' responses monitored and all of these examined as to their implications for the desired goals and objectives. This feedback process should be continuous, although it may well be that modifications will not be other than relatively less frequent – at least that is if the original strategy was in some measure heading in the right direction.

A continuous evaluation of impacts on, and changes in, the market, closes a feedback loop

Of course even the biggest and most often successful companies can get it wrong, sometimes on a spectacular scale, and so it is also necessary that there is a procedure to radically modify direction should the need arise.

There can be little doubt about the earlier statement that *strategy* is the most important activity for senior managers. They must have a full understanding of their customers and their company and soundly based views of possible future directions. Above all of that, they must be constantly checking their vision of the future and ensuring that the strategic decisions are actually delivering the results that satisfy the longer term goals of the company.

Having experienced managerial changes does not mean that the same choices should be made automatically

It normally takes many years to reach senior levels in most organisations but once there the senior people of today must realise even more than others that what was appropriate in manufacture as they worked their way up the organisational structure should not be assumed still to be valid. Such people are subject to the same pressures for change as the rest of the organisation and can show the same reluctance to make that change. For that reason, implementing and managing the change process is a major task and one that we will now move on to discuss in the next chapter.

SUMMARY

- The establishment of a *strategy* is the most important activity of senior management

- *Competitive advantage* positively differentiates your product from the competition making customers wish to own it. Ideally the advantage is not easy for competitors to replicate

- *Competitive advantage* creates *order-winning* criteria which must be supported in a *manufacturing strategy*

- *Manufacturing strategy* involves decisions about *manufacturing processes* and supporting *infrastructure*, and is established in an interactive process with other functional and higher strategies

- Competitive factors can be *qualifiers* – permitting you to be in a particular market – or *order winners* enabling you to gain customers. These can change over time and can move between categories

- The dynamics of competitive strategy greatly affect the process investment decisions

- Senior management are at least as exposed as others in the company to the need for change and must know how to plan for and manage change as an ongoing activity.

5 MANAGING THE CHANGE PROCESS

This chapter considers the crucial questions of implementation of a required new technology. Many companies who are otherwise highly competent have difficulty in obtaining full benefit from a change made for sound competitive reasons. The problems are often managerial or organisational more than technical, but all aspects should be properly considered. We will examine these points through trying to achieve the following objectives:

- Consider the different sources of awareness of the need to change.
- Recognise the multidimensional nature of change.
- Consider the range of change methodologies that are available to managers.

- Realise the importance of early consideration of all aspects of the change programme.
- Consider the use of a framework to guide the decision-making process.

THE CHANGE PROCESS

In any exercise involving major technical or organisational change there is a set pattern of events which can be identified. These events are:

Organisational cycle of change

AWARENESS - ANALYSIS - SPECIFICATION - PRO-GRAMME DEVELOPMENT - SYSTEM TRY OUT - TRAINING AND IMPLEMENTATION - TRIAL - CUT-OVER - EVALUATE - REPEAT.

Some aspects of this sequence have already been covered in this book. Analysis was largely the subject of Chapter 1, i.e. defining what manufacturing had to be good at to succeed in the business environment discussed there. Specification was covered in Chapters 2 and 3 where we examined the new objectives needed to produce the deliverables, while Chapter 3 looked at the particular contributions from selected AMTs.

Awareness and programme development are the subject of most of the discussion in this chapter but before doing that let us briefly discuss the remaining parts of the sequence.

System try-out is obviously appropriate when buying hardware of any kind and it will usually be worth trying out some of your existing material on the new piece of equipment as part of the selection procedure. With some of the softer systems based technologies, a different kind of trial might be more suitable. It may be the case that a pilot project in some small but typical sub-section of the total operation could demonstrate the feasibility of the approach while at the same time 'selling' its benefits to observers. Prior to this, visits to other plants operating in that fashion will be worthwhile and the literature of manufacturing technology and management abounds with information as to the many conferences and seminars.

Most organisations under-invest in training

Once some decisions are made, the development of directed, relevant and timely training for all levels of personnel involved in the change is crucial. Even those companies that do a lot of training always say afterwards that they wished they had done more, while the more typical companies see such training as a device to increase the value of the sale by the system supplier or consultant involved. In fact education is crucial to most of what we are discussing in this book. Ollie Wight, one of the great gurus of MRPII, is credited with the saying "if you think training is expensive, try ignorance!" Unfortunately many of the changes facing managers today are so pervasive in the impact that unless due and careful consideration to the training aspects are properly given and the effort properly financed then the likelihood is that any success will only ever be partial.

Assuming that our company has come this far the next stage is a full trial, perhaps with some parallel working. Parallel working can provide some comfort that the company still has the capability to operate according to the old regime, if the new one develops some unforeseen fatal flaw. There is, however, a downside to this. The people actually involved in making the change will naturally find it simpler to operate in the old ways and may not make sufficient effort to succeed in the new. Thus the decision as to whether parallel working is sensible and, if it is, when to cut-over to total dependence on the new system are difficult managerial decisions.

The final obvious, but frequently omitted, stage is to evaluate the change. This is best done at a number of points in the short to medium term as the early difficulties are worked out and the *Make sure you* system becomes fully operational. It seems incredible that com-
evaluate the change panies who have very tightly defined procedures for project appraisal and financial justification often do not adequately measure the actual outcomes in the same detail that was necessary to obtain the corporate go ahead for the project initially.

Perhaps this is another demonstration of the short-term thinking which dominates many organisations, i.e. once the decision to invest is made the attention turns to the next problem area or supposed panacea. In the same way that the quest for quality is a never ending one then the quest for a better understanding of the nature of the manufacturing system should also be continuing and every opportunity should be taken to learn, record and apply the lessons of the change process for the need to change will always be with us.

Following the evaluation phase it then is important to close the feedback loop and begin the sequence again with, hopefully, heightened sensitivity and useful experience.

Let us now look at the awareness stage in more detail.

Awareness can come from one or a combination of three main factors which can be paraphrased as: *greenfield, into the abyss* and *perceptions of excellence*. Of these, the first two are the result of external influences whereas the third takes effect through the perception of managers, perhaps undergoing the kind of strategic appraisal discussed in Chapter 4.

Sources of awareness – Greenfield, Into the Abyss, Perceptions of Excellence

In setting up any greenfield operation, there lies an excellent opportunity to learn as much as possible about the state of the art in other organisations and emulate or improve on that level. The new location provides the chance to design the complete operation without hindrance through established systems and practices which may or may not have been appropriate to the old business but are unlikely to be wholly suitable to the new situation.

The necessity to consider how best to structure the new situation obliges managers to work through at least some of the options that we have been discussing before making the commitment to particular process and infrastructure decisions.

Greenfield examples

An example of this situation was the company producing gas circulator plant for conventional fossil fuel steam raising plant. Their existing factory was in a city centre location close to its original site and, while some modernisation had taken place, still reflected the company's long history. A change in market opportunity came with the possibility to work on circulators for nuclear power plants but with it came new manufacturing process requirements and quality standards specified by the customer. One possibility would have been to redevelop the city centre site but the greenfield option was more attractive. A purpose built building capable of meeting new cleanliness standards was built nine miles from the original location. A largely new staff was recruited and trained to the higher quality levels needed and different working practices negotiated consistent with the needs of the new operation.

Of course some companies will find it less easy to make this kind of change. The managerial climate and industrial relations experience might suggest in some cases that the greenfield set-up could be an attack on existing agreements (as well they might. if the world has changed faster than the agreement), and as a result organised labour could mount a rearguard action. This seems at least to be part of the Ford situation at Dundee which was seen by one of the union groups involved as weakening the existing agreements in other parts of the Ford UK operation.

Sometimes incoming multinationals or completely new companies have a better chance than long-established ones trying to break the mould. For example, some of the Japanese electronics companies have recruitment policies which aim for young school leavers entering their first employment. The argument here is that such people have not had the conditioning of working in 'traditional' companies and by their youth are also more likely to absorb the required practices of the company.

There might be a concern that greenfield solutions are not so readily available to the majority of companies but if the benefits of simplification and focus in manufacturing apply then one way of obtaining them might well be to think about downsizing an existing operation by breaking the whole into a series of more autonomous business units, in which case the gate to the field might swing invitingly open.

The above situation arises from the realisation that a new market opportunity may be available. The awareness that comes from 'into the abyss' thinking is markedly different.

Into the Abyss example

In this situation a company suddenly recognises that unless they do something fairly dramatic they will slide over the edge and fall to total destruction.

One company in this category was engaged in heavy engineering in a related market to the previous example. They recognised that the competition was global and consistently better at satisfying customer requirements than they had proved to be, although they also had the view that foreign governments did more to subsidise their competitor's prices. With a forecast dearth of home-based business for some years but good prospects thereafter they moved towards a strategy of survival until the return of more favourable market conditions. They still had the competitive issue to address, however. In order to get the process going they had to convince everyone in the company of the severity of the threat. Everyone had to look long and hard into the abyss and then begin the work to fight their way back from the edge. Parties from all sections of the company visited competitors world-wide and brought back the message and the measurements of how uncompetitive they were and a major re-investment, re-structuring and re-organisation was put in place over a number of years. The essence of what they had to do was the decision to bid for contracts on the basis of the cost performance they were targeting some two to three years out and then aggressively, but with company wide involvement, set about achieving the targets.

Currently they have achieved the cost reductions but need to react again to competitors' actions. They are still very aware of the dangers but are perhaps not so close to the edge as they once were while having a much more modern capability to continue the struggle.

Perceptions of Excellence

Perceptions of excellence come about through stimulation to find out what others are doing. It is hard to understand how apparently successful managers would be unaware of what their competitors are doing but one of the problems in manufacturing has long been the focus on the immediate and the reward in fire fighting. It is only relatively recently that companies have realised that there is a real need to modify the ways in which manufacturing is regarded. To this end there has been an increase in government exhortation, increased conference activity and publication, and a whole new section of the travel industry has developed to organise study tours of some exemplar organisations.

By definition you, as a reader of this book, do not fall into the class of blinkered manager but there is still a natural human tendency to see such developments as not necessarily suitable for application in one's own environment. Often, too, the problem may lie in another manager's lack of awareness, perhaps too often those whose 40 years' experience is more like 1 year repeated 40 times. Perhaps a quick look into the abyss will do the trick but it would be nice to take action before that became a real possibility.

Individual middle managers cannot always be expected to change the culture of a whole organisation but efforts can be made to present a case to the senior decision makers as to possible implications of actions or inaction. Of course if this is done following a request from the top it becomes easier to suggest new ideas, since there is at least some interest already established and the power and political situation is more obvious and, hopefully, manageable.

There is a danger however that the Western tendency to go for the quick fix, fad or flavour of the month might create a desire for some new AMT without a full recognition of its contribution to competitiveness. So let us be sure that along with the awareness goes adequate analysis.

PROGRAMME DEVELOPMENT

The individual views, perceptions and experience of the senior decision makers shape and influence the response to a need for change.

Harold Leavitt (1964) proposed a framework of four interacting variables as shown in Fig. 6.

In the terms of the discussion here we can define the task as the chosen mission for the manufacturing unit, i.e. the particular set of required ouputs to support the company's strategy. We have been arguing that greater competitive pressures are suggesting that this is likely to require at least some modification, if not necessarily a complete abandonment of an activity. The logic of the above figure is that in order to achieve the desired modification to the *task* we should be considering the balance of effort devoted to making changes to the other factors involved. Since each interacts with the other, the programme of change must consider carefully each aspect in relation to the others.

Many AMTs impact people and structure as well as technology and task

Here is where the backgrounds of the senior decision makers are relevant. They need to be aware of the choices they have in creating the balance between these factors and fundamen-

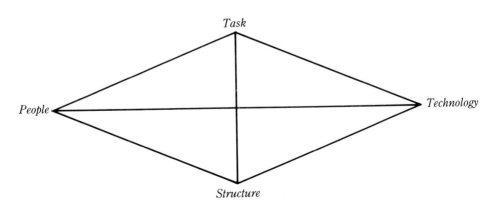

Fig. 6 Leavitt's entry points for organisational change

tally recognise that many of the AMTs discussed here impact greatly on *people* and *structure* as well as the more obvious *technology*.

Technology has often tended to be considered the realm of the specialist but this must now be put into its strategic context. Making changes to the technology of manufacture is likely to require modifications to the skills and job designs of the people. Such changes will also call into question existing patterns of responsibility and authority, as well as physical flows of data and materials.

A fragmented, functionally oriented approach to changes at any point in the linked structure of factors will tend to produce at best a sub-optimum result and at worst a dangerously unbalanced edifice liable to collapse at the first signs of increased load.

Some of the impacts of change might be foreseeable but others may evolve over time following a change. It is for this reason that companies need to have mechanisms to recognise a disfunctional situation arising and to have an appropriate toolkit of responses available. Huczynski (1987) has attempted such a task in describing nearly 300 organisational change methods. In so doing he defines two dimensions to enable a classification to take place (Fig. 7).

Some of the change targets we can consider as prime in our attempts to improve our manufacturing task, whereas others we might see as more likely to become targets because of some failure in the balance achieved.

For example, *clarifying roles, improving communications, redesigning work, motivating employees, creating conditions of excellence* all have immediate relevance to the discussion here. Aspects of *encouraging innovation* could be useful in the context of small group improvement activities in support of total quality management while *managing the environment* suggests possibilities of control over the supply chain.

The other change targets, i.e. *managing differences* and *addressing intractable problems* fall more easily into the category of coping with outcomes from the kind of change programme considered here.

The other dimension highlights the view that managers have what might be described as a dominant orientation or propensity to look for the solutions to organisational problems in the same

CHANGE TECHNIQUE FAMILIES

CHANGE TARGETS OR PROBLEMS	TECHNICAL	STRUCTURAL	PERSONNEL MECHANISMS	LEADERSHIP	PEOPLE
Clarifying roles		Responsibility charting Functional role analysis Multiple job holding	Affirmative action Realistic job previews Assessment centres	Likert System 4 Reprogramming MAPS approach	Executive family seminar TA Job support
Improving communications	Electronic mail Satellite training	Forcing device Worker directors On-going feedback system	Briefing groups External mirror Suggestion schemes		Information sharing meetings Interviewing Drawings
Re-designing work	Factory of the future Quality of work life Office automation	Job enrichment Telecommuting Networking	Core working Flexible manning Harmonisation	Assessment Centre Interaction management	Career planning Decruitment Outplacement
Motivating employees	Group technology	Employee rules Team appraisal M60	Discipline without punishment Reward systems Wellness programme	Behaviour modelling Management by walking about Situational leadership	Coaching Counselling Stress management
Creating conditions for excellence	Quality management JIT	Quality circles Business teams Union-management committees	Company culture Recognition awards Mission cards	Managing for productivity Theory Z management Excellence training	Norm modification Quality awareness training Concept training
Managing differences		Alternative dispute resolution Ombudsman Mini-trial	Relations-by-objectives Let's talk it over programme Sensitivity bargaining	Grid management LIFO FIDO	Confrontation meeting Third party peacemaking No lose conflict resolution
Encouraging innovation	Delphi technique Brainstorming Factory of the future	Collateral organisation Intrapreneurial group Skunkworks	Follow-up Intrapreneurship	Behaviour modelling Synectics	Smart process
Addressing intractable problems	Nominal group technique Delphi technique Brainstorming	Multiple management Temporary task force Forcing device	Consultation Shadow consultant Consulting pair	Kepner-Tregoe Action learning Resources management	Creativity techniques
Managing the environment	Globalisation Network organisation Investing in a small company	Exporting for others Two-way contracting Linked sub-contracting	Workforce reduction Customer interface contracting Staff exchange	Vendor excellence awareness	Merger management

Fig. 7 Organisational change methods – from Huczyuski (1987)

related family of techniques. These are really just expansions of the Leavitt framework referred to earlier to encompass *technical, structural, personnel mechanisms, leadership* and *people*.

The dangers in such patterns of thought are obvious and we have already discussed a tendency to treat the manufacturing area as one where the technical specialists make the decisions, sometimes without an awareness of the strategic impact of what they choose. Any narrow approach to such situations must, however, tend to create problems in the longer term since the aspects of the situation not considered by such a focus must surface sooner or later.

This Western tendency to see things in closely defined little boxes is not the way in Japanese companies who spend, in our eyes, an inordinate amount of time discussing, in minute detail, every aspect of a decision, taking input from all sections of the company, before implementing quickly. Fig. 8 shows the relative proportions in the two cultures.

The Western pattern also fails to take account of the ways in which freedom of choice is constrained over time and therefore how the costs of making changes as a result of problems, only identified during implementation, will tend to rise. Fig. 9 shows the conflicting trends over time.

This shows that early on the choices are unconstrained but as time elapses earlier decisions begin to reduce freedom of choice as well as making any required changes more difficult to effect and therefore more costly. This is simply a function of the interconnectedness of a manufacturing business so that small changes will tend to create the need for other changes in more remote parts of the company which have some kind of systems connection. It is also the case that the earlier we are in any sequence of linked decisions the greater is the potential to make significant improvements to the total system.

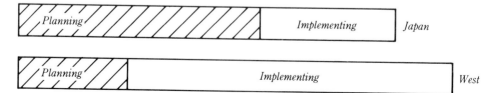

Fig. 8 Time allocations in Japan and the West

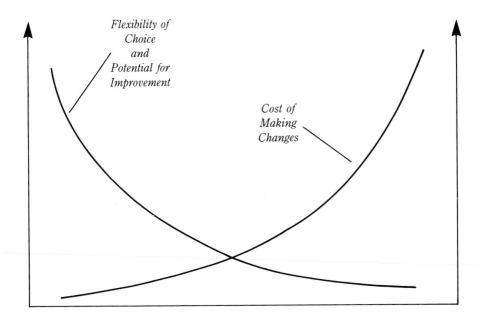

Fig. 9 Conflicting trends of flexibility of choice and potential for improvement against cost of making changes

This same relationship is relevant to the *total quality control* discussion, in that effort devoted to product and systems design reduces the costs of conformance monitoring and equipment adjustments later.

This discussion therefore leads to the conclusion that a programme of technical change in the manufacturing area has to be developed in an environment where all of the potential problem areas are considered in advance and suitable procedures put in place in anticipation rather than perpetuating the wasteful firefighting behaviour normal in the Western manufacturing manager.

As already discussed, many of the AMTs are not simply techniques complete in themselves. Behind many of them lies a need to question basic assumptions and patterns of behaviour and often the underlying attitude of the people. Since each new technology requires the involvement of some people, even if in the limit these are merely systems designers, installers and maintainers rather than operators, it is in the end their behaviour that has to be modified.

Many AMTs require that someone's behaviour be modified

Many organisations have long experience of changing priorities coming in messages from senior management. If one of the more fundamental, company wide AMTs is to be properly introduced the people have to believe that the senior management really mean what they say. Companies who decide to recognise the supremacy of good quality, even over material production, have to demonstrate that they are actually prepared to stop the plant if a serious quality problem occurs. Unless this can be done, the lower level people will see the quality statement as a hope rather than a strategically important criteria.

In the same way, a company's measurement system tends to communicate messages of the importance of different criteria. Thus it is nonsensical to develop JIT sourcing relationships with suppliers and then continue to measure the buyers on their ability to switch suppliers in search of marginal reductions in unit purchase price, when to do so greatly increases the total cost of the acquisition because of the many downstream costs adversely affected by a hasty change in the supply base.

Individual cycle of change

Thus, not only must the complete change process be thought out, planned and implemented, it must be done in a way that everyone affected must be able to identify with, connect into and want to operate under. We must therefore design the change programme in a way which takes account of the need for individuals to go through a cyclical process of *awareness, understanding, commitment, action* and *improvement*.

RESULTS THROUGH ACTION ON PURPOSE, PEOPLE AND PROCESS

One approach which has been found to give good results has been documented as The Technical Change Audit by the author's colleagues Boddy and Buchanan (1987).

The essence of that approach is defined in the title of the decision framework used to help the various kinds of 'stakeholders' involved in a technical change identify with and plan a major exercise in this area. This is the *results through action on purpose, people and process*, abridged to the RAP-3 Framework. Within each of the three sections we have three categories of concerns to examine and manage. For the purpose section, these are *strategic focus, positive policies* and *kit to fit*. The people section covers *work organisation, management style* and *support systems*,

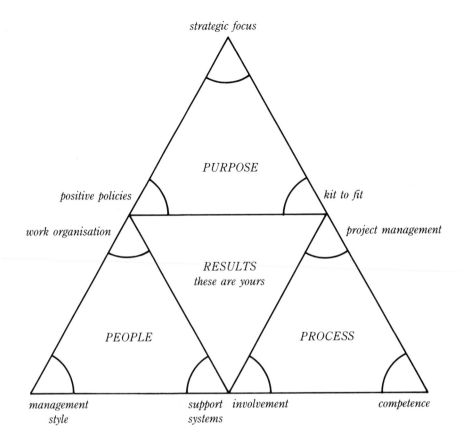

Fig. 10 The RAP-3 Decision Framework – from Boddy and Buchanan (1987)

while process includes *project management, involvement* and *competence*. This is shown in Fig. 10.

Purpose

The *strategic focus* argument recognises that there are two categories of approach for managers implementing technical change. The first is an internally oriented concentration on control and efficiency. This is almost the stereotype for a narrowly focused engineering solution to a manufacturing decision. What must be realised is that many AMTs have innovative potential. That is to say that the eventual best use of them may not be apparent when first installing them. It follows, therefore, that those managers aiming to improve decision making capability and emphasising the impact on the market position effects of the AMT will tend to produce a more significant result and it is this that the framework helps to identify. This is to some extent what this book is all about.

Positive policies also fit well into the message so far. It is necessary to support a strategic focus with policies on training, recruitment, responsibility, rewards and financial appraisal which help and do not hinder attempts to decide on the basis of external effectiveness rather than internal efficiency. The short-termism of Western companies has already been mentioned but if we look at normal Japanese investment criteria we can see the difference. The Japanese will tend to be operating at much lower interest rate levels, certainly nowhere near the artificially high levels some commentators have argued against. They will also tend to accept longer payback periods, and if it is justified on the basis that it is a new technology about which it is necessary to learn and to gain experience of, then this will overrule the financial concern.

Kit to fit covers the concerns expressed earlier in the book about the contributions that the various AMTs can make to the competitiveness of the business. At that time we concentrated on whether a particular technology would be able to satisfy our requirements. We must also take account of who will be supplying the kit since there is much that a supplier can do to help or hinder a successful implementation. Once the equipment is operational we also need to be concerned that it will continue to function as planned. Often the future is so uncertain that one criteria for selection will be the ease of modification or upgrading should circumstances require. Here again the tendency for Japanese companies to develop their processing equipment in-house reduces their dependence on a supplier's rate of change.

People

Work organisation recognises that new technologies affect the kinds of jobs that people do and how those jobs are organised into groups. It also identifies the choice in some AMTs to replace or complement human skills, although we have been arguing here that the latter is the route to continued improvement at least where there is still a role for mental ability. The final consideration in this section is a consideration of how to win people over to the need for change, which covers aspects already covered here under the awareness heading. It also considers the political and power factors which can intrude into many aspects of organisational life.

The *support systems* factor highlights the role that the manufacturing and other organisational infrastructure can have to aid or impair the success of a new technology. Of course some of the AMTs discussed here fall naturally into the category of support systems themselves but it is still relevant to consider whether the other support systems are truly supporting the business objectives.

The *management style* factor recognises that in our context many AMTs require a fundamental reappraisal of the role of a manager and some would tend to argue for the removal of at least the junior and often the middle ranks from the scene. Whether this is in fact desirable is debatable and the solution, like so many others, is likely to be very company specific. Where these managers do remain, the likelihood is that they will cease to be disciplinarians and order givers and become much more advisory. This has of course major implications for the organisation in its recruitment and training of such people. Greater access to on-line information also changes the way in which managers operate making them both better informed when making decisions and more visible once they have done so. Greater variety and more rapid response to customer requirement also increases the potential stress on such individuals.

Process

For any major change in the organisation, success is more likely if a *project management* structure is put in place with a planned team membership working towards defined objectives and with effective monitoring of performance.

Involvement in the process of change is fundamental to the ability of individuals to 'connect' and identify with the change. The involvement of people at all levels must be catered for. Here again the Western tendency for decisions to flow down from the top and problems flow up from the bottom should be recognised. Fig. 8 highlighted the different approach used by Japanese companies where involvement has the appearance of being total as they strive for complete consensus.

Competence argues for training, at all levels but for different purposes, to ensure that the chosen technology has the qualified support of people eager and prepared to use it properly and to realise the innovative potential it will have if we have chosen wisely.

The RAP-3 Framework, then, provides the fundamentals of a complete consideration of how we can develop a programme to implement our chosen AMT and successfully manage the change process – with some confidence that the many and varied interests of the personnel of the company have been properly considered and that the final plan will tend more towards a easy implementation rather than one fraught with problems, reappraisals, negotiations and ever-increasing cost. Unless we can confidently proceed in this direction then all of the good things offered by the AMTs might as well not be there, since we will not be able to make use of them whereas our competitors might.

SUMMARY

- Awareness of the need to change can come from three main directions, i.e. *greenfield, into the abyss* and *perceptions of excellence* – which create their own problems and opportunities

- Any technical and organisational change involves the four interacting factors of *task, technology, people* and *structure*

- In developing a programme of change, managers tend to assume that only some of many available change methodologies are valid based on their previous experience. This will lead to problems during the implementation phase as these other considerations come into play

- Greater effort devoted to planning can reduce the amount of time needed for implementation and reduce the overall time considerably

- Choices made early in the cycle cover a wider range of possibilities and can have greater impact than ones made later which also are more expensive to modify

- A programme of AMT implementation based on the RAP-3 Framework aims for *results through action* on *purpose, people* and *process* and provides a way of considering all of the relevant factors in a constructive way

6 LESSONS FROM THE INDUSTRIAL FRONT LINE

In this chapter we will draw on some of the experiences of companies who have made attempts to implement some of the AMTs discussed here. To do this, we will firstly consider those factors which often seem to go hand in hand with, and even cause, a failure to gain full advantage from such a change. We then have to think about those things a company must do to ensure that whatever benefits have been obtained are not dissipated through negligence in the future.

Workpeople are seldom antagonist to new technology

There was a time when the normal expectation of the likely reaction to new technology of ordinary work people was that such developments would automatically be resisted. This has of course happened in a certain few well-reported cases, of which the newspaper industry is the most famous. The reality for most companies is not universal hostility from the work people – in fact the reverse seems often to be the case.

There is nothing inherently threatening about AMTs, at least over the short term. Within manufacturing industry, greater automation has tended to reduce the requirement for unskilled manual work while increasing the demand for technical skills in system designers, supervisors and maintenance personnel. In fact the job displacement effects of reducing competitiveness is usually recognised as more potentially serious than new technology while the remaining jobs are often more attractive than the ones displaced.

In the West, the outcome of such job displacement is regarded as society's problem rather than the company's one. Only relatively few companies see their commitment to their employees as longer than the immediate need to buy some of their skills.

A recognition of the new ways of thinking about people as a resource for the future as opposed to a current factor of production would tend to reinforce positive attitudes towards innovation and change in manufacturing. Thus a manufacturing business moving towards the new enlightenment is unlikely to encounter severe problems from its lower level staff. Middle and sometimes senior staff may be a different matter, however.

The role of, and requirement for, middle managers is most likely to change

Many of the traditional activities of middle managers can be regarded as non-value-added operations, i.e. directing, disciplining and controlling wayward workers; collecting, analysing and reporting results; requesting, chasing and supporting service staffs in operational problem solving. Many of such activities will be redundant under an AMT regime, so what do we do with these people? Some will still contribute to the development of the remaining staff but their contribution must be carefully analysed.

Thus we can see a situation where, to revert to an earlier analogy, the troops are keen to tackle the enemy and thereby keep the home fires burning, but the staff officers and some of the generals are still fighting the last war using the tactics which served them well then but are not necessarily suited to the mobile, guerilla, hit-and-run approaches which allow bigger success to build on many smaller campaigns.

What is it that tends to go wrong then? What are the lessons from the front line?

What follows is a discussion of nine common types of problem which can produce less than satisfactory results and two situations which can limit the scope for further success.

LACK OF VISION

Countries and companies with long-established trading relationships tend to suffer from a form of reduced peripheral vision which hinders their ability to perceive potential threats from outside their normal sphere of operation. This same disregard for threat seems also to affect their perception of opportunities.

The classic example of this is the British motor cycle industry which chose to ignore the enormous market for small machines growing up in Japan to concentrate on internal industry fights, thereby permitting the Japanese to build up home market volume before targeting British and American markets with devastating effect.

The lessons of that case are in fact varied but for all its datedness there is much that is relevant to many industries today.

This inward focus on existing markets is a feature of American companies simply because of the enormous size of that market, so that American firms have to be very large before they will need to look outside of Continental America for growth opportunities. Enormous markets are attractive to others of course and it is no accident that the bulk of Japanese offshore investment is into America.

This form of parochialism affects American multinational operations overseas whose managers complain that head office does not recognise the complexities of having to cater for highly differentiated markets demanding different products, standards, packaging and language features.

Within the UK the problem has been one of only slowly recognising the implications of having relinquished control over an empire on which the sun never set. The new opportunity and threat of a truly common market in the European Community is so little perceived that a major advertising campaign is needed to awaken managers from their complacency.

The tendency towards an overly introverted approach is only seriously challenged when the foreign competition makes significant inroads into formerly secure markets, and by that time it may well be too late to mount an effective defence.

There would also seem to be a tendency to only see potential competition from within an existing industry sector, but here again the global market suggests that companies from different backgrounds can develop capabilities if the opportunity is attractive enough. The nature of technical change in materials alone suggests that traditional companies may have competition from unexpected quarters. On a more immediate timescale this is already happening in the rapid development of Pacific Rim, South American, Indian and Chinese industrial capability.

Along with a wider view of the possible markets and competitors there is also the need for a wider view of technical potential in a range of industrial sectors. Here there has to be a concern for the rate of investment in pure research. At a time when the UK Government is calling for greater relevance to immediate industrial applications and a real cut in expenditure, the Japanese are increasing the rate of their investment in the basic sciences which they foresee forming the foundation of future industrial activity.

The lesson to be drawn from this is simply that the role of the senior management team has to be redrawn to emphasise that managing the path to the desired future is the real purpose of such people and that more junior levels should be empowered to handle current operations.

LACK OF SYSTEMS AWARENESS

The Western tendency is to sub-divide and categorise in minute detail any task which is then attempted by groups structured in essentially the same way. This is perhaps a legacy of the *scientific management* approach but it also seems to be ingrained in our culture. Our educational systems reinforce this by teaching subjects in isolation from one another with occasional attempts to provide some form of integrating study, usually quite late on in the course.

This pattern is repeated in our career structures where the decision to follow a particular path is often taken at a rather young age and the progression is along that career path whose logic is not so much need-driven as tradition-founded and historically reinforced. Thus the Engineer is an Engineer (with much sub-division within that career) and is normally trained in a rather narrow specialised domain. In similar fashion, someone in Personnel is unlikely to have an ongoing commitment to any other functional area. The list goes on and emphasises the singular nature of career structures for most company personnel. This makes it difficult to move people across functional boundaries without major upheavals.

This is the pattern in the bottom nine tenths of the organisational structure. At the top the requirement is different, however. Suddenly we need generalists who can understand, communicate and empathise with a variety of specialists but what have we done to prepare them for this task? Often the common denominator of money suggests that the most appropriate person is one who is comfortable with the financial aspects of a company's business, but the training of Accountants is not any more or less all-embracing as any of the other professions and the likelihood is that they will not be comfortable evaluating technological matters.

Thus we have the majority of companies composed of people whose education, training and experience is often discipline-based and thereby not well suited to taking an overall view of the business.

There can be little doubt that we must redress the balance in some way.

The requirement is to understand the integrated systems concepts of a business to the extent that an understanding is obtained of the various interactions, flows, influences, decision points and outcomes. In this way the true implications of actions can be realised, evaluated and modifications incorporated before the actions are initiated. Going through such a process is likely to shift the pattern towards the Japanese model in Fig. 8 and thereby reduce the total time by reducing implementation problems considerably.

The lack of systems awareness manifests itself in many ways, but one of the classic examples relates to the different perceptions of marketing and manufacture in relation to sales order details.

To the salesman an order for 100 different items at $1 each is the same as an order for 100 identical items at $1 each, but this is manifestly not the case for manufacturing (unless of course manufacturing can operate totally flexibly with zero set-up and change-over time). This is perhaps an overstatement to make the point, but were it true an order could be taken in good faith by the salesman who might in fact be creating an impossible task for manufacturing. Thus what makes good sense in one part of the system is not good for another part and is often not good for the initiator either, since an impossible task guarantees failure.

A salesman who had worked in manufacture would not readily accept the first order without checking whether it could be completed as required by the manufacturing group. Similarly, a management system in hardware, software or procedures could enforce the checking of capability before making such a promise to close the sale, but only if there has been the systems awareness to so design the system in the first place.

LACK OF A STRATEGY

The British have some telling phrases in their language which provide an insight into national traits. "Muddling through", "it'll be all right on the night", "the gifted amateur" are all examples which indicate a propensity to accept what is given and make a virtue out of 'coping'.

In a highly competitive environment, 'coping' is not sufficient. If all a company can do is react then it will never be in a position to control the high ground in the battle and will always be fighting rearguard actions.

Strategic thinking is different from normal operational modes and creates the need for different data and analysis tools. We have argued that the financial and marketing people have been better at this than manufacturing.

The same argument that says top level vision and systems awareness is needed follows that by saying that this must be incorporated into a formal approach to ensure adequate discussion and agreement from all sections of the company.

Large companies are perhaps more likely to have the personnel to undertake this kind of activity but they have to guard against an overly bureaucratic structure impeding communication.

Managers can still make decisions about issues which have

major strategic potential based on little more than a feel for the situation. Of course there will always be a role for the intuitive aspect of an experienced manager when his experience is relevant but it must be better to have decisions informed with as much relevant information as is sensible.

One Managing Director was being asked to consider the purchase of a CAD system for the design drawing office of his engineering company. When asked to show how the equipment would support the company's strategy, his response was informative, if a little alarming. His view was that his company was simply a jobbing shop in a particular sector and could therefore not have a strategy as such. The justification for the purchase was based on the fact that other similar companies in related market areas had already purchased such systems and therefore his company should purchase something to 'keep up'.

To this end he sanctioned an expenditure of around £50,000 to purchase a single workstation for learning and evaluation purposes. At the time the workstation route to CAD was only just becoming viable and so the expenditure limit constrained choice considerably. In the event, the young graduate tasked with the equipment selection made a good choice and the installation proved successful according to the subjective opinions which were all they were able to go on.

After a year the company was in a situation where the designers were keen to obtain the benefits of the technology but could not get sufficient access to the machine which, while it had impressed some customers with the quality of the output produced, had not in any measurable way contributed financially to company results.

The Managing Director was now in the position of having to make a decision about expanding the CAD facility to satisfy the perceived needs of the design office – but what equipment should be considered?

A new definition of requirement might have suggested different equipment (perhaps to cope with increased data volumes or communications to other systems) but what of the experience gained in the operation of the pilot kit, should that simply be discarded? The decision was made to go for more of the same and this did work out successfully.

The important point in this example is that failing to take the strategic view of the first equipment purchase permitted a situation where the expansion decision was in fact circumscribed by that first decision. The longer term picture was largely deter mined by an evaluation done at a time when that longer tern possibility was not adequately built into the original equipmen specification. It is not surprising, therefore that such decisions can lead to situations where opportunities are missed because of existing facilities which are not as fully suited to the new re quirement but cannot easily be changed.

FAILURES OF ANALYSIS

The same fragmentation that produces people ill-prepared to take a systems view of a situation also creates a tendency towards incomplete analysis of a technological situation. Two examples will help to illustrate the problem.

The first is of a company who spent £500,000 on a CAD/CAM system one of whose justifications was to automate the genera- tion of NC tapes for their many machine tools. A system was selected, installed and good results obtained from the CAD side, but CAM proved more of a problem. This revolved round the need to be able to specify standard tooling to the CAM database to enable the productivity savings to be generated during NC programming. It was only at this point that the company realis- ed that they had no standard tooling. In fact they had tools for just about every job they had ever done in every variation im- aginable but the designers did not know what was available, and would not have known what to do with such information had it been available. In effect they did their own thing and the tool- ing engineers then built or bought as required.

To move to a system of standard, easily interchangeable tool- ing was then costed at around the same total as the CAD/CAM installation itself, but no one had considered that during the analysis leading up to the system specification.

Interestingly enough, the manager responsible for tooling had long been arguing the case for standardisation, but he was regarded as a troublemaker and universally ignored by the power structure in the company at that time. He certainly was not consulted during the system specification and selection pro- cess.

The other example shows the same tendency to look for solutions from too narrow a viewpoint. Here a company producing electric motors decided to automate an area which was highly dependent on the availability of skilled armature winders. The job was to wind a suitable grade of wire onto a stack of steel laminations and to position the free ends of wire within the slots of the copper commutator pressed onto the end of the laminated rotor.

The engineers finally selected a machine from a Italian supplier after demonstrations at the manufacturer's plant with sample rotor stacks. Everything looked fine until the equipment appeared on the shop-floor and continually failed to produce anything of significance in spite of highly qualified troubleshooters standing by.

What had happened was that the sample stacks were not representative of the normal quality levels achieved in normal production, and the machine simply could not cope with the variability in the dimensions and orientation between the slots in the commutator and those in the rotor stack. This variation did not impact product performance in any way and the people operating the normal winding machines were very adept at coping with the variations and producing a product within its performance specification. The outcome was that this expensive piece of high technology was mothballed for some years until further developments in the process control of the steel lamination presses allowed a consistent flow of material to be established to cater for the automated machines' limited acceptance range.

Both examples illustrate the 'little boxes' mentality and a failure to recognise that the analysis phase benefits from a wide perspective of views and experience.

FAILURES OF INADEQUATE TRAINING

Training and general levels of education have already been discussed as a problem at all levels in many organisations, but this is compounded when new technology is introduced into a company.

Companies consistently underestimate the amount of training needed and the timespan over which support will be required.

Many of the AMTs force a change in skill patterns needed to properly operate them, so that kind of training must be provided. It must also be timed so that the users actually gain experience at the point of use and not theoretically with no opportunity to practice and experiment. Others in the organisation need different kinds of training appropriate to their needs to interface with the new system or simply to understand how the business is changing. This suggests that some of the training must be up front to support a successful introduction, but there will also be a requirement for ongoing updating and phasing-in of new people.

In some of the systems-based technologies the training is not so much about how to operate the equipment as an education and behaviour modification programme to cope with new ways of thinking and working.

The key in this is, as discussed in the last chapter, is to so tailor the training process so that people can see the relevance of what is being taught for their immediate circumstances. In the words we used before, people have to 'connect' with new ideas and want to give them a good try.

FAILURE TO FOLLOW THROUGH

Allied to a training failure in general terms, is this kind of failure where the message of change has been communicated to all in the organisation, but the message has in some way not been fully understood or accepted in a more remote part of the company.

This can also be a systems-related problem since the appropriate modifications to reward or measurement approaches have not been made.

A number of companies introducing JIT into the sourcing set-up have accepted the need for increased amounts of cooperation with suppliers and that unit purchase price is not the sole criteria on which a supplier should be measured. Nevertheless, cost reduction in the long term is still a powerful competitive factor (all other things being equal), and if the buyer acts as the main contact with the supplier, and he presents an image of wanting price reductions all the time, then the message received by the supplier can still be that price overrides everything. In fact many such buyer companies are trying to define a total acquisition cost to account for quality and delivery considerations, support costs and other aspects of the buyer/supplier relationship. It is also the case that supplier selection is increasingly a team effort from financial, technical, quality and delivery viewpoints. This creates the situation that the buyer no longer has the power he once had to switch suppliers to get the benefit of a marginal price reduction. Suppliers do not necessarily understand the full impact of the change in the relationship and may still see the interest in cost reduction as a reversion to the old adversarial, bidding down the price approach they have suffered under for some time before.

It is therefore not enough that senior management agree to a new approach – it is necessary to ensure that the follow through reaches all parts of the organisation.

FAILURE OF STRUCTURE AND INFRASTRUCTURE

For all that, the argument for increasing the focus on a manageable set of tasks for manufacturing has been around for a number of years, many companies find it difficult to put this into practice. Partly this would seem to be because of the belief that expensive equipment must be fully utilised and so work is sought from wherever available in order to keep the plant busy.

The same company discussed earlier as an example of success after 'looking into the abyss' fell into this trap a few years later when they attempted to break into an emerging high technology market. The market situation was such that the demand outstripped the capacity of the normal smaller companies geared up to satisfy it and the customer looked to companies like our example who could contribute. Unfortunately the smaller companies had set a pattern of prices suited to the scale of their operations but not ideal for larger units. The freedom to negotiate a better return was not there since all of the larger companies had excess capacity which they wanted to utilise. In theory, a collaborative agreement between the companies (even if not entirely legal) could have raised the price overall, but the companies were fierce competitors in other lines of business and so our company simply bid for the work at the going rate.

They then made the classic mistake of trying to produce for

this market using exactly the same facilities, structures and systems as for their normal business. In particular their financial controls did not make it possible to separate out these different business areas, and since they were competing for the same manufacturing facilities, while the company still regarded this activity as peripheral to their main business, it became increasingly difficult to perform to the customer's expectations.

To make matters worse the company had no way of knowing how much it was actually costing them to produce this new product. (Since the margins were initially very tight there could now be no possibility of actually making any money on the deal.)

It was only when a special investigation was mounted that the need to separate out these different activities was fully understood and a form of 'plant within a plant' was instituted to complete the rest of the orders.

Another company had a long and typical pattern of computerisation from early beginnings in accounting-related areas and had a well developed data processing function. As part of a needed upgrade of their hardware, the supplier bundled an attractive deal on MRP software which seemed a good idea to the Financial Controller and the DP manager. The software was widely used, the supplier highly reputable and the modular nature of the software seemed a sensible path to follow. Unfortunately the software was developed for use in a highly repetitive environment while the company was really in a make-to-order situation with the additional requirement for full traceability of all parts and processes which did not feature anywhere in the new system. The company then made all the other mistakes of inadequate training, faulty analysis and bad data, and failed completely to take account of the human and organisational changes needed to support such a major change in its infrastructure.

Four years after the initial start on this project the system was still little more than a generator of shop paperwork, while no one trusted what the system told them and physically checked everything.

SUB-OPTIMISED MYOPIA

One of the main aspects of systems theory is the possibility that what is demonstrably ideal for one part of the system actually impairs the performance of the system as a whole.

Concentration on equipment utilisation is one example of this where what can be measured easily is closely controlled, but the effects produced by that policy are not so visible or so easily quantified and so are assumed to be positively related to the controlled item. In many of these relationships the outcomes are in fact inversely related, but this is not always fully realised by non-manufacturing people.

A more extreme example of this problem is shown by the case of a company who had made major changes to the manufacturing philosophy incorporating CNC, AGVs, FMS and JIT.

The company then became involved in a leveraged buy out from the holding company. One of the requirements of this was to generate suitable income streams at just the right time in the process of the buy-out for it to succeed. The effect of this was to force a concentration on the profit margins of the operation such that some business was rejected due to insufficient margin, and yet the original reason for the reinvestment programme was to protect market share as well as revenue against very hostile global competitors.

This process also tended to support older patterns of behaviour. For example, the *purchasing* function began to search the World for cheaper sources of materials and components. This has lead to the situation where one assembly visits four countries before reaching the plant.

The manufacturing people do not regard this as progress and are worried by the impact on quality or delivery performance. As the Plant Manager put it "OK, we know that they (Purchasing) are supposed to take account of a vendor's performance but the numbers are hidden. There are measures of *returns to vendors* but it doesn't cover for the pain we feel down here if it goes wrong. He's all right, he looks good with a cost of material reduction of 95% of plan but we are still suffering."

This is an example of short termism in the extreme but the message going to their suppliers will take a long time to change if they do revert to their former development path.

More generally, there is a question about the traditional ways in which accounting is carried out. This is largely still based on a count of direct labour employed but with increasing levels of automation the numbers of such people are on the decline and why is it important anyway? There was a time when the majority of the cost was attributable to the direct workers but that has long ceased to be the case. In many companies, materials costs outweigh direct labour by 2 to 4 times and the ratio of indirect workers will show the shift to staff, knowledge workers. (Note however that this category will be greatly affected by many of the AMTs).

This results in measures which, particularly in investment appraisal, tend to emphasise direct labour saving to justify investment, although the operation of accepted appraisal procedures can be improved to take account of these concerns.

There is also a move towards accounting based more on the throughput of material and recognising that fully implemented JIT might operate with very few material transactions, as suppliers are only paid when the finished goods leave the plant to go to the final customer, rather than on receipt of every delivery or invoice.

Such developments recognise that the purpose of an accounting system internal to the company is to aid the decision-making process. This can only be done if the accounts are designed to suit the needs of that business as it evolves. Unless managers ask for information to be gathered and analysed in ways appropriate to their needs, the accountants will default to normal patterns established by convention over too many decades.

This kind of accounting is after all only score-keeping – someone else should be defining the rules of the game!

PROBLEMS OF MAINTAINING MOMENTUM

One of the continuing problems of the Western tendency to see things in terms of 'the quick fix' is that there is a built-in expectation that attention will shift to the new 'flavour of the month'.

Much of what we have been talking about are not passing fads but journeys to manufacturing excellence, even if what is appropriate for a particular company at a stage in time is not as theoretically pure as the guru's would have us believe was necessary.

Continuing journeys of this kind are not the normal expectation of Western managers. Even the need for life-long, continuing education is one that is far from universally recognised. In this climate then, it is important to build in aspects which in a sense renew the vigour of the campaign from time to time and re-commit the organisation to pursuit of the desirable goals.

This would certainly seem to be a requirement of major quality improvement programmes and a similar need was found in one company when moving towards JIT operations. This was a large multinational whose geographically diverse sites tended to have a product mission covering the whole of the operational sector, i.e. about a third of the globe.

The JIT message was taken onboard the manufacturing arms of the company and significant improvements made across a number of factors, but let us select time as one of the important ones: manufacturing controlled lead times reduced from being measured in months to a matter of weeks for supplied materials, and hours for actual manufacture. This was all very well for a time, but there seemed to be no real impact on company performance.

What was happening was that the distribution system for this enormous trading area and the information system creating orders on the manufacturing sites were not as advanced as the manufacturing units in their thinking. In effect the manufacturing arms' customer was another part of the same organisation whose stock holdings and inertia meant that for all of the excellent progress inside manufacturing the real customer was not receiving the benefits.

Concentrated effort was then made to modify distribution patterns, stocking policies and information systems to try and improve the capability to match that of the manufacturing plants, but in the meantime attitudes in those plants began to change. In effect they had suffered some pain to make changes but had not seen the benefits promised. In such situations it becomes difficult to maintain enthusiasm and momentum.

The lesson to be drawn here is that many of the AMTs are so system-wide in their impact that attack on all relevant fronts is required. This puts into question those who advocate that there is a preferred sequence of introduction of approaches such as JIT in that, for example, internal company JIT should be fully implemented before moving out to managing suppliers and customer information. This misses the timescale effects of such developments and omits the benefits from a widespread improvement in many of the company's operations by activities in all sections of the business. Had our example company gone for the simultaneous approach then the interruption to the momentum would not have been of the same magnitude.

What has been discussed so far are some examples of things that can go wrong in practice. The next section relates to factors which follow having had some success.

SUCCESS IS NOT ENOUGH

Success is important to people and it is important to present opportunities for people to succeed in obtaining their targets. There is a basic problem, however, that we have alluded to before. If we set impossible targets we must by definition fail, but perhaps in striving for the impossible we travel a little further past the point at which the impossible once started. A question of balance then enters in. Impossible tasks, if they are seen from the beginning as impossible, can create a disincentive to strive for them but setting targets that are easily obtained do not provide the same scale of opportunity. If we also have a culture that does not recognise the value, in learning terms, of some degree of failure, we then create a situation where the relatively safe, assured target will be the one at which we aim. This can lead to a kind of creeping incrementalism which will probably not be enough to redress serious competitive threats. Setting aggressive targets forces a consideration of radically new approaches which may in the end prove more advantageous than the more of the same, but slightly better, ways of old.

It becomes one of the tasks of the senior management to foster a spirit of adventure where the effort of trying hard but failing is not punished but is seen as another possibility to develop an increased understanding to permit a higher likelihood of success at the next time of trying.

We therefore should be looking for chances to make a success of a project as a motivation to look for more, but to see the real objective as one of continually raising our sights to higher and higher targets and measuring our progress towards them as the really important indicator of success.

The experience of *quality* measurements indicates this pattern. For many years we were content to measure the possibility of failure in percentages, i.e. parts per hundred, but decreasing size and increasing complexity in electronic components forced a move to a measure of parts per million and now the latest requirement is to move to parts per billion.

The logic is inescapable. Even with the tiny probability of failure implied by such as 100 parts per billion, the shear volume of opportunities for failure in highly complex products with hundreds of thousands of parts means that the possibility of some failure in the complete product is simply unacceptable. Thus moves to produce large scale flat panel liquid crystal display television screens to hang on the walls of our homes are totally dependent on quality levels unimaginable even ten years ago.

ENVIRONMENTAL SCANNING AND COMPETITIVE EVALUATION

Given that the competitive situation is one of constant change, often at what appears to be an increasing rate, it becomes a necessity for globally competitive companies to keep a very watchful eye on developments in related and, at present, unrelated areas.

As discussed before this should be part of the strategy formulation phase, but it is also important to consider not just what markets are doing but also to establish what the competitions' manufacturing functions are trying to achieve.

It will be of interest to establish how far the competition is along the path to excellence since this may open up possibilities for their marketers to change the strategic thrust in some way built on their manufacturing capability.

In a similar way, basic technologies and sciences will be under investigation and development in laboratories around the world and information will often be available for those suitably motivated and informed to search for it.

After all, this is precisely how the Japanese started – by licensing and copying Western technologies. Now the pattern is reversing with Japanese patenting activity outstripping all others in many sectors. They also are switching resources into the basic sciences, rather than development for immediate market opportunities – since they recognise that it is from such basic research that the products and industries of the future will emerge.

While the large Japanese corporations and their imitators continue to pose a threat to the major companies of the West, smaller companies would do well to look to their laurels. As the

Japanese move into the USA and Europe they are looking for suppliers who can work to the same standards as they are used to at home, and while some have risen to the challenge the window of opportunity will not remain for ever open. Already we have seen moves by Japanese supplier companies to follow the majors off-shore and continue the symbiotic relationship. Such a relationship is likely to prove a barrier to entry for indigenous companies which might well prove insurmountable.

SUMMARY

- There is only limited evidence of Luddism in work people but rather more evidence of a potentially disastrous introspection in senior managers which is also linked to an inability to perceive the systemic effect of decisions

- Many of the failures to effect adequate change is reflected in inadequate planning for all of the details of the change

- A major problem is the use of inappropriate accounting measures and a failure to look to the longer term to produce systems geared to the requirements of the business as it evolves

- Major innovations need constant re-invigorating and re-emphasis or the attention will shift to the latest fad

- Success lies along the path of continuous improvement but if a target can be achieved along the way this will help motivation wonderfully

- Companies must have at least some of their corporate antennae tuned to the wider scientific and industrial scene to become alerted to future threats and opportunities

7 CONCLUSION

This book is a reflection of the re-appraisal that is underway in manufacturing companies as they react to increasing competitive threats from around the World.

There will be perhaps very few instances where manufacturing is the sole source of competitive advantage. In fact the reality is that no one function on its own can provide this, since the essence of the argument is that we must improve our ability to perceive of the total system as an integrated, interdependent and intercommunicating entity.

The role that manufacturing has to play then, is to provide support to the objectives of the business and to deliver what the customer wants in a way that enhances his satisfaction and helps provide a confidence in the ability to deliver satisfaction whenever it is requested in the future.

In order to do this, companies need to re-discover, and re-define the manufacturing role in the particular market and environmental situation in which that company finds itself.

This role will be defined in terms of actual specifications of required performance in the factors of *quality, delivery* and *cost*. These words of themselves cover a wide range of sub-factors which cover everything from product concept and design, through all the stages of supply and manufacture, and on through the distribution chain to the ultimate customer. Depending on market requirements, these performance specifications can be more or less variable over the normal operating timescale of the company, although all companies must recognise the need to plan for and properly implement change.

The re-examination of the ways in which manufacturing can provide the desired outcomes, causes us to think very seriously about some of the assumptions and guiding principles which have served for so long but must now be replaced by new paradigms. These new ways of thinking are so fundamental that it is worth repeating them here as they form a new blueprint for decisions about the nature of a manufacturing system into which Advanced Manufacturing Technologies can fit.

APHORISMS FOR THE NEW MANUFACTURING

- Customers are your future – get close to them.
- Provide a flexible response to customer needs.
- Suppliers are your life blood – nurture them.
- Take a total systems view – along the whole supply chain.
- Aim for effectiveness not efficiency.
- Simplicity before complexity – people before machines.
- Design for function, form and effective manufacture.
- Avoid waste – add value not cost.
- Do it once and do it right.
- AIM FOR CONTINUOUS IMPROVEMENT.

Some of the AMTs discussed here contribute in different ways to the achievement of these desirable situations and an attempt was made to classify them against the *manufacturing deliverables*. This should not be regarded as a table simply to be consulted and decisions made accordingly. It was merely an attempt to indicate the nature of the analysis that companies should go through in evaluating the contribution that a particular AMT might be able to provide. Note that it is a company decision, not one solely for the engineers – not unless the engineers are working to a specification which has received widespread consideration by a technologically literate group of people from other functional areas. This is simply to counter the natural tendency for technologists to be excited by the prospect of involvement with a new technology for its own sake and this may not be in the complete business interest.

The contribution from AMT is only one aspect of a wider consideration of the strategic needs of the company. This should be part of a continuing programme of activities operating to an agreed procedure, and evaluating input from all sections of the company.

Here the concepts of *order winning criteria* and *qualifying criteria* can help the debate between Marketing and Manufacture to aid the specification of the things that manufacturing have to be good at and for how long they should follow that path before another change is indicated.

Making the required changes is probably even more difficult than identifying what it is that needs to be changed. The management of change and its active encouragement within the company's culture is one of the big jobs senior managers have to do. One particular framework based on *results through action on purpose, people and process* has proved useful in practice and covers some if not all of the difficulties, recognising as it does that change takes place within a complex environment of information, political and power processes, as well as the formal aspects of organisational life.

All in all, manufacturing is at an interesting stage of development. Never before has it been receiving the attention it is getting at the moment.

Of course the increased import penetration in manufactured goods is a contributing factor, but it is not too many years ago that influential people were arguing that it did not matter that nations did not actually manufacture all or indeed a large proportion of their total requirement so long as somehow they could generate sufficient income to pay the going rate in the market. To these people it was a natural consequence of being early into the industrial revolution that entry into a post-industrial state would also come quickly.

Unfortunately this scenario poses some problems.

There seems little reason to suppose that what has happened in manufacturing could not also happen in some of the traded services, and a nation which is generating large surpluses on its manufacturing account is in a stronger position to influence world economics than one whose strength might be more historical and supported by time zone geography. After all, British manufacturing once led the World and even in 1951 had around 25% of World trade in manufactures, now it is below 9% (of a larger total) and falling.

Of course, not all services can be traded but there are many that are capable of expansion almost indefinitely if money were available to pay for them. Trade in manufactured goods offers an opportunity to generate that income and increase the standard of life for more of the people.

In similar vein, the developed world has a responsibility to help the less-developed nations of the World help themselves to a better future. In so doing they would not be doing themselves any harm. Greater prosperity provides new market opportunities and the possibility of a mutually supportive spiral.

The chance is there to reflect on the lessons of better competitors who have demonstrated the impact companies can have once they have a manufacturing system truly capable of taking on the World. They have done it by recognising and developing the skills that people have to create improvements by attention to detail in all areas of activity and by recognising the strategic impact that this process can have on competitive advantage. They have also recognised that change is the new name of the game and the companies that manage the change process are the ones to beat in the marketplace.

If this book has encouraged you to start or re-double your efforts to take advantage of the possibilities offered by Advanced Manufacturing then it will have served a useful purpose.

The author wishes you well on your journey.

You will need intelligence, information, application, good colleagues and a deal of luck, but all our futures depend on you making the effort.

8 FURTHER READING

Chapter 1

The literature of *quality* is long established and some of the major authors are being re-discovered in the West following the belated recognition that actually putting theory into practice creates an awesome force for competitive manufacture. Notable writers include:

Feigenbaum A V (1983) **Total Quality Control** (3rd Ed) McGraw-Hill, New York

Deming W E (1982) **Quality, Productivity and Competitive Position** MIT-CAES, Cambridge, Massachusetts

Juran J M (1974) **Quality Control Handbook** (3rd Ed) McGraw-Hill, New York

Crosby P B (1979) **Quality is Free** McGraw-Hill, New York

Crosby P B (1984) **Quality Without Tears** McGraw-Hill, New York

More recently Japanese writers have published in the West, most notably:

Taguchi G (1986) **Introduction To Quality Engineering** Asian Productivity Organisation/IFS, Bedford

Taguchi G (1987) **The System of Experimental Design** Asian Productivity Organisation/IFS, Bedford

Shingo S (1985) **A Revolution in Manufacture: The SMED System** Productivity Press /IFS, Bedford

Shingo S (1986) **Zero Quality Control** Productivity Press/IFS, Bedford

Shingo S (1987) **The Sayings of Shigeo Shingo** Productivity Press/IFS, Bedford

The concept of a balance between supply lead time and customer demand lead time has been differently expressed by:

Mather H (1987) **Logistics in Manufacturing** Institute of Mechanical Engineers, London

Chapter 2

For an insight into Japanese manufacturing, the two articles below provide a good starting point:

Hayes R H (1981) 'Why Japanese factories work' **Harvard Business Review** July/Aug, 57 – 66

Wheelwright S C (1981) 'Japan, where operations really are strategic' **Harvard Business Review** July/Aug, 67 – 74

Schonberger's books were major factors in causing us to re-appraise our thinking to emulate Japanese success:

Schonberger R J (1982) **Japanese Manufacturing Techniques: Nine Hidden Lessons in Simplicity** Free Press, New York

Schonberger R J (1986) **World Class Manufacturing: The Lessons of Simplicity Applied** Free Press, New York

The principles of Optimised Production Technology also challenge basic thinking in a fundamental way:

Goldratt E M and Cox J (1986) **The Goal** Creative Output Books, Hounslow, Middlesex

A good overview is provided by:

Hartley J (1986) **Fighting the Recession in Manufacturing** IFS, Bedford

Chapter 3

It is difficult to suggest suitable readings for this chapter given that each AMT has a literature of its own. Nevertheless the following points in the right direction. Note, however, that some AMTs are covered in other sections.

ACARD (1983) **New Opportunities in Manufacturing: The Management of Technology** HMSO, London

Corke D K (1985) **A Guide To CAPM** Institute of Production Engineers, London

Gallagher C C and Knight W A (1973) **Group Technology** Butterworths, London

Groover M P (1980) **Automation, Production Systems and Computer Aided Manufacturing** Prentice-Hall, Englewood Cliffs, New Jersey

Groover M P and Zimmers E W (1984) **CAD/CAM Computer Aided Design and Manufacturing** Prentice-Hall, Englewood Cliffs, New Jersey

Halevi G (1980) **The Role Of Computers in Manufacturing Processes** Wiley, New York

Hartley J (1984) **FMS at Work** IFS, Bedford

Institute of Production Engineers (1983) **A Guide To CAD-CAM** I Prod E, London

Institute of Production Engineers (1986) **Flexible Manufacturing: A Guide** I Prod E, London

Ingersoll Engineers (1985) **Integrated Manufacture** IFS, Bedford.

Kochan A and Cowan D (1986) **Implementing CIM** IFS, Bedford.

NEDO (1985) **Advanced Manufacturing Technology: The Impact of New Technology on Engineering Batch Production** NEDO, London

Orlicky J (1975) **Material Requirements Planning: A New Way of Life in Production and Inventory Management** McGraw-Hill, New York

Ranky P G (1986) **Computer Integrated Manufacturing: An Introduction with Case Studies** Prentice-Hall, Englewood Cliffs, New Jersey

Voss C A (1986) **Just-in-Time Manufacture** IFS, Bedford

Wight O W (1981) **MRPII: Unlocking America's Productivity Potential** OWL Publications, Williston, Vermont

An attempt to highlight the convergence of the various streams of technology was made by the author as:

Macbeth D K (1985) Flexible manufacturing – The hope for European industry **European Management Journal** 3(1), 27–32

Chapter 4

Strategy from a corporate, business point of view is a rich area of publication. This sample is therefore no more than that.

Porter M E (1980) **Competitive Strategy** Free Press, New York

Porter M E (1985) **Competitive Advantage** Free Press, New York.

Quinn J B, Mintzberg H and James R M (1988) **The Strategy Process: Concepts, Contexts and Cases** Prentice-Hall, Englewood Cliffs, New Jersey

A very useful view of Japanese strategy is provided by:

Ohmae K (1983) **The Mind of the Strategist** Penguin, Harmondsworth

In the manufacturing area, Skinner is the seminal writer and his book draws together his major contributions:

Skinner W (1985) **Manufacturing : The Formidable Competitive Weapon** Wiley, New York

Hill T (1985) **Manufacturing Strategy** Macmillan, Houndsmills, Basingstoke

In the general British context see:

Bowman C and Asch D (1987) **Strategic Management** Macmillan, Houndsmills, Basingstoke

Johnson G and Scholes (1984) **Exploring Corporate Strategy** Prentice-Hall International, London

For a global view of Manufacturing Strategy developments see the various reports from INSEAD, for example:

De Meyer A, Nakane J, Miller J G and Ferdows K (1986) **Flexibility: The Next Competitive Battle** Working paper 86/31, INSEAD, Fontainbleau , France

Chapter 5

The four variable framework was first proposed in:

Leavitt H J 'Applied organisational change in industry: Structural, technical and human approaches' in Cooper W W, Leavitt H J and Shelley M W (eds) (1964) **New Perspectives in Organisational Research** Wiley, New York, 53–71

For a complete view of the variety of organisational change methods with comment, further readings, etc., see:

⅄ Huczynski A A (1987) **Encyclopedia of Organizational Change Methods** Gower, Aldershot

Fig. 7 is taken from :

Huczynski A A (1987) 'Performance through intervention using organizational change methods' **European Management Journal** 5,1, 49–56

Fig. 10 is adapted from :

Boddy D and Buchanan D (1987) **The Technical Change Audit: Action for Results No.2 The Diagnostics Module** Page 45, MSC, Sheffield

A useful set of readings is provided in:

Rhodes E and Wield D (eds) (1985) **Implementing New Technologies: Choice, Decision and Change in Manufacturing** Basil Blackwell, Oxford

Chapter 6

The example of the British Motor Cycle Industry is included in a book of readings:

Bignell V, Dooner M, Hughes J, Pym C, and Stone S (1985) **Manufacturing Systems: Context, Applications and Techniques** Basil Blackwell, Oxford

A major exponent of the need for change in the accounting profession has been Kaplan, see for example:

Kaplan R S (1986) 'Must CIM be justified on faith alone' **Harvard Business Review** March/April, 87–95

For further examples of problems see:

Shaw W N and Macbeth D K (1986) 'Strategy and tactics of managing advanced manufacturing technology' **Proc. 3rd Int. Conf. on Human Factors in Manufacturing** IFS, Bedford